THE
BRAVE
CHILD

THE BRAVE CHILD

A tale about the treasures in life

Andreas Hartinger

The brave child

A tale about the treasures in life

Copyright © 2022 Andreas Hartinger

ISBN: 9798798637409

Cover Design: Creative Studios

Translated from German by Vera Filthaut

Contact: andreashartinger@protonmail.com

For my sons…

Life offers us a lot of treasures. Some are hidden in this book. May you find them and make them your own. Trade them wisely throughout life's journey, where ever you may be at the time.

Contents

CHAPTER 1

Courage

...or fear? You choose your companion!

W hen I first bumped into the boy, he was resting under a big oak tree, wearing an old linen shirt that was patched in many places and short leather trousers, as was customary in the villages at the foot of the mountains. The soles of his feet were as black as the ace of spades, with his elbows and knees showing scratches that had witnessed daring juvenile antics. He was tired and discouraged.

Tired because he had missed out on his sleep last night and discouraged because it had suddenly dawned on him what he had let himself in for.

Beads of sweat rested on his forehead, for it was a hot summer's day. So hot in fact, that one would have wanted to jump into a cool pond and go for a paddle, just as ducks would do. But there was no pond and no ducks for that matter.

Only a dusty path leading up from the south, right from the bottom of the mountains to the nearest town in the north. You could see the sparkling facades as well as smoking chimneys looming in the distance. Looking in the other direction, dry grassland stretched from east to west, so dry that it almost burned your eyes.

Next to the little boy lay a wooden stick he used as a walking cane and knotted to the very end of the it hung a small bundle of provisions. *That must be his luggage,* I thought. *I wonder what he keeps in there? What would a little boy like him need on his travels? Probably a few apples, and maybe something to drench his thirst, and a straw hat to shield himself against the glistening summer sunlight. Maybe also a little wooden horse his father carved for him and a handkerchief to wipe the dust out of his eyes.*

And as I was pondering about the contents of his little bundle of possessions, I suddenly noticed that the boy was sobbing heavily.

What's this… I thought. *How can anybody be so sad on such a beautiful day?*

And then, as I looked at him, I saw *it*, the reason for the upset. I already knew it—it had always been my adversary.

The grown-ups called it 'Fear'.

I, however, look upon it as a fat old toad that torments with its plaintive croaking, but when addressed, quickly disappears.

All it needs is for someone to address the situation.

The boy did not stir. His hands firmly pressed against his face; he was not making the slightest attempt to stop the toad from taking over. So, I decided to step in and help him along.

I raced over to the oak tree, and whilst doing so, created an angry swirl across the thin summer meadow. The toad, startled by the noise, flared up its nostrils, inflated its body and quickly disappeared into the long grass.

"There you are, boy. This is how to deal with a toad," I said.

The boy dropped his hands into his lap and looked at me, blind from the tears streaming down his cheeks.

"Thank you," he said. "Thank you for helping me. But who are you?"

"Well, I have many names and many faces. Every child sees me differently. But if you really want to know… They call me *Courage*. The grown-ups call me *Courage*."

"*Courage*? That is indeed a very strange name," answered the boy, and wiped his tears away. "Are you from that land far away?"

"Well you know, I am at home here, there, and everywhere and I am always around when children get sad and upset. Just as you are now," I answered.

"It sounds nice to be able to have a home here, there, and everywhere. All I have managed to do so far is leave mine and get as far as this oak tree."

The boy started to cry again, but then he suddenly straightened himself out and pushed his worries away. "The town over there looks quite intimidating to me," he said. "I have never been in a big town before, and don't quite know how I will get on once I get there."

I could sense the feelings of despair inside the boy's mind and decided to keep him company for a while. I sat next to him and started telling him about some of the funny things I had encountered in life, such as the day I met a kangaroo that preferred to hop around backwards, just because it could, and deemed it funny. I told him about the donkey that climbed high up into the trees every night just to be able to watch the stars. And not to forget the little chimpanzee that used to wear a banana skin on top of its head.

When I asked the chimp why, it simply answered: "I like it. I like the way the ends curl over. Quite decorative, don't you think?"

I told the boy story after story about the funny and often magical things our beautiful world has to offer. The little boy liked it. He laughed and laughed. The serious cloud of darkness that had darkened his little face had long gone, and we laughed and joked for most of the afternoon, even forgetting about the searing heat.

The boy seemed pleased to have met me and when our bellies started to rumble, he opened his little bundle happy to share what was left of his provisions "Here. I have two apples left and I would like you to have one, so please take it. From now on, we shall be friends."

I smiled. I had been right with my line of thinking. I thanked the boy and made him a promise. "From now on, I will be your friend and accompany you to wherever life takes you."

And thus, after devouring an apple each, we walked

towards the town, singing all the way. I cannot quite remember the songs we sang, but what happened next will never be forgotten, not ever, and it shall be an inspiration to all those who are tired and discouraged, to do just as the little boy did.

CHAPTER 2

Fate

...is what they will call it, once you are done

The path widened, as we got closer to the town. The thin bridle path quickly changed into a well-trodden clay path with even more joining, until finally they all turned into wide streets, leading to where people longed to be. If you looked at it from a bird's-eye view, you would have been able to spot a vast network of paths streaming into one, reminding you of a set of veins just like you can see on the back of your hand, which then eventually turns into one thick aorta. An aorta pulsating with activity — becoming the heart of the town.

You could already hear the pumping and pounding from a long way away. It was impossible to miss, even in the dark of the night.

Darkness had caught us out whilst we were happily

walking along, singing and whistling. A quick look over our shoulders showed us that we had covered a lot of ground, for the mountains and meadows behind us had shrunk into little cones and patches.

The boy had told me what had made him leave his home and he spoke honestly about the reasons. As open as children are, he did not hold back. It was not because of his parents, nor his upbringing. Oh no, he came from a good home.

He had been raised in what he and many others would consider to be a *paradise*. At least that's what he called the little farmhouse at the bottom of the mountains, where his father and mother looked after the family together and farmed the fields just like his grandfather and great-grandfather before them. The little farm had been in the hands of the family for generations. The fields provided enough crops to feed the hungry mouths, there was even enough to keep a few animals and make a couple of guineas every year. Life was simple and rewarding.

The boy and his three siblings could chase through nature as much as they wanted, and if they ever had a falling out, their caring mother's soothing words would quickly bring them back together.

Life in the little farmhouse was governed by love and laughter. Until one day, when they had a visitor from town. "Grow or go!" the tycoon said to the boy's father without even battering an eyelid.

"But why would we?" asked the father. "We have everything we need. It is not right to take from nature just for the sake of greed. To take more than necessary is not good at all. The land will not be prosperous if you drain it."

"Well, you may stick to your philosophy, Mister, but be warned. I will have bought all the surrounding farms in the valley before the year is up."

The man pulled a gold case from his pocket and lit himself a fat cigar. And whilst he puffed on his cigar with a certain amount of satisfaction, an evil grin appeared on his face.

"My customers in town pay me good money for the goods produced in the countryside," he said. "Therefore, you have two choices. The first one is you become like me, but you will never be able to do that. The second is that you start working for me, and to be allowed to do that, you will need to sign your fields over to me."

And just as the evil man had spoken his last word, the father could no longer contain his anger and lost his temper, using words his four children had never heard before. As the air turned blue, he pushed the unwanted visitor out of the house and shouted, "Get out. Get off my property! There will be no changes here!"

Afterwards he hid his bright red face in the arms of his wife, for he did not want his children to see him upset. The boy, equally upset, ran after the evil tycoon and shouted, "There will be no changes here. And you… you just need to get lost."

But feeling intimidated by the large man, he was only able to mutter those last words.

The man stopped and dropped his cigar onto the clean floor, squashing it with the heel of his boot.

"Just wait you silly boy, you have no idea. You are

just the same as your father. But I know what I am doing. I have learned those things in town, and that is why I will always get what I want."

He jumped into the awaiting carriage and disappeared further into the valley where the other farms were situated.

After that fateful day, normality only seemingly returned to the family and their little farm. Especially the mother tried her utmost to restore peace in *paradise*. The three little siblings had soon forgotten and carried on laughing and joking, but the father seemed very quiet and subdued, and the boy was old enough to understand that his father was suffering under an enormous burden. And thus, the mood travelled from father to son. And none of it was their fault.

Then, suddenly, the boy could hear that voice again. *Grow or go. Grow or go*, almost as if it was eating him up inside.

Night after night, he suffered bad dreams, accompanied by thousands of nagging questions. And on top of it all, he could hear the toad croaking. The situation seemed hopeless. Were they about to lose everything? Was the world really that cruel? The boy felt not only helpless, but he had also lost all hope, so much so that he thought his heart would stop beating. He could not bear to see his whole family destroyed.

All of this, and the loud croaking of the toad, were enough to drive the boy out of the house with just a bag of apples and his little walking cane.

That fateful night, he had briefly woken his oldest sister and told her that he would be leaving. He wanted to try and find a way to save all that was dear to him.

He asked that his parents would not be cross with him and vowed that he would come home as soon as he had found all the answers to all the questions. Then, and only then, would he return.

"Alright," his sister had mumbled, and seconds later returned back to sleep. The boy took his cane and climbed out of the window next to his bed, heading towards the town without looking back.

I had no right to judge the decisions the boy had made. To evaluate whether it was right or wrong to exchange a loving family for a world full of risks and danger. It was my job to stand by him for as long as he would need me to.

There are always challenges in life and the first one was just about to start.

We had entered the outskirts of the town where rows and rows of identically looking little houses with equally small gardens had been build. Shops and workshops however were scarce.

"I'm hungry," said the young boy, "and tired. My eyes feel just as heavy as my legs."

I could see his fatigue. He stumbled more than he walked, he was that tired. It was time to try our luck and search for a night shelter.

Right in front of us stood a building with a large sign above the door. A golden horse indicated the entrance to an old inn. Written underneath, in blue letters, it stated the name of the premises: "The Coachman's Inn". The ground floor was brightly lit.

Glasses clinked, punters laughed, and someone was

playing a harmonica. Some of the guests were enjoying the evening, talking about the events of the day, whilst others had already bedded their heads on the soft pillows in the guest rooms on the first floor. If you listened carefully, you could even hear their snoring from where we were standing, outside on the street. "Don't be frightened," I said to the boy, "just knock on the door."

The boy straightened his shoulders, lifted his head and stepped towards the big wooden door with its iron rivets. *Knock-knock*. But his fist struck the door gently, almost as if he was stroking it.

The clinking of the glasses, the laughter and the harmonica continued all the same.

"If you want to attract attention, you will need to make a little more noise," I said to him.

Knock! Knock!

This time, his little fists hammered against the door. Silence. The laughter and the music suddenly stopped. You could sense how countless pairs of eyes had all turned towards the door, wondering who dared to disturb their entertainment so late at night.

Not so long afterwards, we could hear the floorboards creaking under the approaching steps of someone seemingly very heavy and the iron bolts sliding back from the locks inside the door. The door flew open, and the landlord appeared, his shirt sleeves rolled up, his big head glowing bright red and an enormous gut bursting from underneath a golden waistcoat.

"What do you want? Should you not be in bed?" he snarled at the little boy.

"Good evening, sir," said the boy. "I have been travelling from far afield, and I am looking for a bed for the night and also a little food. I don't need a lot; a horse box would do if nothing else..."

"Well, I suppose there is room in the stable for you. But it will cost you. One silver coin. Everybody who stays here pays a silver coin. It is not cheap to run such a noble inn."

I could tell straight away how the towering man blocking the doorframe was sensing lucrative business.

The boy answered him honestly. "I do not have a penny to my name. Forget about the food, and I am sure the horses won't mind me..."

But the greedy landlord would not listen. It was pointless. The little boy had not even finished his sentence when the door was noisily thrown in his face. Bang! The first bolt slammed into the lock.

The guests inside returned to their clinking glasses and laughter and the harmonica continued without further ado.

I shook my head and pointed down the row of houses. "There must be a space somewhere. It is just a matter of finding it."

But that matter proved more difficult than first thought. At the next house, a young woman opened the door, one child in her arms, another hanging onto her leg and a further four dirty mouths behind her. "I am sorry," she said. "I cannot help. I can only just feed mine and my husband is not even back from work yet."

We carried on walking and knocked on the door of

the next house that still had lights on.

Unbeknown to the little boy, I could see how a curtain brushed aside, and then suddenly the lights went out, pretending that no one was around.

What a strange place. Probably better not to spend the night there anyway.

So, we carried on searching and searching and all we got were refusals, excuses and cold ignorance. The glass palaces and chimneys of the big town were coming closer and closer, and the boy grew more and more desperate. We needed to find something soon in this little suburb, or we wouldn't stand a chance. The town centre with its anonymous streets didn't offer much hope. To top it all off, I could hear that toad again. Thus, I encouraged the boy to try one more time. It was the last house anyway.

Right at the end of the road.

The yellow light of the street lanterns showed this house to be much smaller than the other already quite small and uniform ones. But it seemed as though there was a generous garden surrounding the little house. And behind it, even though it was difficult to spot in the dark, there appeared to be what looked like a luscious meadow.

The air smelled of sheep, and if there were really any sheep around at all, they would have long gone to sleep. As we walked through the wrought iron gates, I looked up and on the gable, I saw two iron turtle doves with their beaks touching.

Knock! Knock!

With his fists still firm from all the previous attempts, the boy hammered against the door. And …nothing. We were about to turn around and wave farewell to the turtle doves when a light came on in the window to the right, followed by another in the room next to it, accompanied by the creaking sound of an old wooden door. A little old lady peeked through the gap, her appearance just as I imagined the grandmother of Little Red Riding Hood to be.

Silken grey locks peeked from under her beautifully embroidered sleeping cap. A pair of little round wire glasses rested on her fine-cut nose and her body was covered with a snow-white nightgown, the edges set in lace. Her bare feet stuck snug in bulky, but seemingly very cosy felt slippers.

"Hello, little boy. All alone on such a dark night? Who sent you?" she asked, not even the slightest bit cross about the late disturbance.

"No one," answered the boy. "I have left home. It's a long story and entirely my own decision, but I am tired and hungry now, and it seems that I will have to rest my head on the coble stones tonight."

The boy was searching for the best words he could find. He knew that this was his last chance, and he was trying to charm the old lady into letting him stay.

"On the pavement?" the old lady shrieked. "Absolutely not. Who could be so cruel so late at night. Come on in child, quickly, come on in."

The boy felt the warmth that radiated from the old woman. He trusted her in an instant and did not hesitate to enter the house.

Not even an hour later, with a belly full of food, he was snuggled down in a soft, warm bed with an enormous feather duvet pulled right up to his nose. He was dressed in a clean linen shirt, which the old lady had pulled from the depth of a large trunk.

There was a glass of fresh milk on the bedside table, and next to him on the windowsill the old lady's cat looked down on him contently.

"She normally sleeps in here all on her own," said the old woman. "She will be pleased about the company."

The boy nodded and asked his host for her name. "I am very sorry, I nearly forgot, after all the excitement," he said.

"They all call me *the old weaver woman*, because I can make many a fine thing from the wool of my sheep. You may leave the *old* out and just call me *the weaver woman*."

"That I will do," answered the little boy, and he started to thank her for all the good things she had done for him that evening.

"That's quite alright," the woman interrupted and smiled. "A nice day will be awaiting us tomorrow. Just you wait and see. I am very much looking forward to it. Now close your eyes and try to rest."

If you had been watching from the street, you would have noticed the lights go out in reverse order to the way they had come on.

First the boy's room, then the corridor and last the room of the weaver woman. It was the first time ever the little boy spent a night away from home.

A first night away from his parents, his siblings and all the things he held dear to his heart.

I thought about the weaver woman, listened to the purring of the cat and watched on as the silence of the night provided them all with a good rest. I watched as his duvet slowly rose up and down in keeping with the rhythm of his breathing, and how he briefly frowned, as if something was haunting him. But it was only a brief bad thought, soon pushed aside by a good one as he drifted into a deep sleep.

What adventures did life have in store for him? Where would his journey take him? These were questions the boy did not care about at that moment; for he was fast asleep.

CHAPTER 3

Health

...comes first, always

The first rays of sunshine gradually permeated through the window, bathing the end of the bed in bright sunlight. Very slowly, they crept up the sparkling white covers, eventually reaching the boy's face. His ears, eyes and nose were still the only parts of his body that peered from the thick feather duvet.

The rest of his body was snuggled away, resembling a hibernating tortoise.

A thin ray of sunshine began to tickle his nose, gently at first, but then, when he didn't stir, becoming a bit more persistent. As this also proved to be in vain, this one ray summoned up more rays for assistance. The boy awoke to a familiar tickle in his nose, his nostrils flared and just before even more rays could race to help, there was a thunderous sneeze. *Atishoo!*

The boy sat upright and looked around, astonished and a bit lost. *Where am I?* he wondered and rubbed the sleep out of his eyes.

He let his eyes wander around the room, taking in the white walls and the furniture. Next, his little hands felt the soft nightshirt he was wearing, and then he felt the iron springs of the mattress and started pushing them up and down until they made the mattress wobble.

Meow! There was a sudden sound from the left.

The cat glared at him with piercing eyes, trying to make him understand that she was in charge in this house, and was not at all amused about having been woken up so early. She stretched and arched her back before jumping off the bed and making her way to the door to call her human.

Soon, the door opened, and the weaver woman stepped into the room.

"Good morning, you two," she said cheerfully. "How was your night?" And then without even waiting for an answer, she continued, "Oh, dear, I see my darling is starving. Time to get up! The day is not going to wait for us."

She rushed over to the window and opened it wide. The sweet morning air entered the room.

She put some clothes out for the little boy and briefly stroked his frizzy hair before she left.

Her voice kept going in a little sing song citing the day's work.

"Up when the cockerel crows, to bed when the sun

goes. Feeding the animals with hay and straw, working the loom for evermore, cooking, combing and having a bite, ready to work through until night" she sang as she walked towards the kitchen.

The boy sat in his bed with his mouth wide open. Never ever had he seen such a bundle of energy. And most definitely not with white hair and this early in the morning. He watched her with childlike curiosity and let the happiness transfer over to him.

Breakfast consisted of bread, nuts and warm milk. Then it was time to get out into the fresh air. But what else would a little boy do anyway? The garden here was not what you would expect it to be. It was not as uniform as all the others in the street. With no fenced-in lawn, a little paradise stretched far beyond the tiny house, much bigger than one would have expected. They wandered around it all morning and the little boy helped the weaver woman wherever he could. Feeding the chickens and the sheep, collecting apples and picking herbs from the herb garden, fetching water from the crystal clear creek which originated from a natural spring somewhere in the garden. And because water always finds it natural way it had created many bends, taking little turns here and there, and where it hadn't carved bends into the dark fertile soil, it had created soft verges and riverbanks covered in shingle that glistened in the sunshine.

The boy found great joy experiencing all this, but he also had to think about his siblings and how nice it would be if they could see all of this too.

The old lady noticed the upcoming cloud darkening

his thoughts and asked, "Well, what do you think? Do you like my little abode?"

"It is all very nice here," answered the boy.

The old woman smiled and bent down to pick up a fallen apple. She rubbed it on her apron and passed it to the boy. Watching him, I could see that there was a question on the tip of his tongue which he almost didn't want to ask.

At the same time, I could hear the hoarse croak of the toad in the background.

That toad had found us again. It was thriving on the embarrassment one feels when someone is lost for words in the middle of a conversation.

But this time, just before the toad could take over, I had already whispered into the boy's ear.

"Just ask, boy. Just ask. A well-meaning person will never make fun of you."

The boy cleared his throat.

He gathered his thoughts and as he opened his mouth, the annoying croaking stopped.

"How come you have such a beautiful plot of land right in the middle of this suburb, even though all you seem to own are a couple of sheep and a few chickens?"

The old woman looked at him in astonishment and also a little bewildered, but then she smiled.

"No one has ever asked me that," she said, "but I will try and answer your question."

They made their way back to the house, where they separated the collected fruit into the larder and then sat together in front of the loom by the lounge window. Here, the weaver woman showed that she knew her trade, using her foot to lift one half of the warps. Every second warp thread was lifted with this step, creating a triangle. She shot the shuttle through the triangle, lifted her foot, combed the wool down and repeated this same procedure over and over until all the wool had disappeared from the shuttle and the little boy handed her a full one.

By the time the cloth had grown, the boy had learned that the weaver woman was in fact one of the oldest occupants in the town. She had lived in her little house since long before the suburb even existed, just like her parents before her. At that time, the noisy, grimy town had not extended its borders as far as they reached now. There had been no smoking chimneys or sparkling glass facades. Just a few farms scattered here and there: their farmers breeding cows or sheep. But soon the town had run out of space and tried to gobble up everything that interfered with its growth. The wonky cobblestones made way to a tarmacked road and the farms and farmers were forced to make way for houses and shops, pubs and inns. Gaslit street lanterns started sprouting like mushrooms, to be lit by a night watchman every evening. The weaver woman however, kept hold of the farm after her parents died. She continued breeding her sheep and refused to give into any urbanisation that was coming her way.

At the same time, she started fighting the industrialisation of her beautiful surroundings. She saved every sovereign and every guinea she could spare from her earnings received for her splendidly woven cloths. She did not earn many riches, but she was always there when one of her neighbours sold up in order to exchange their scythe for a hammer. And thus, her once tiny property got bigger and bigger and eventually turned into a little paradise.

And of course, all of this did not happen without the envious and the scoundrels, those who wanted to make a quick buck or two. The old lady spoke of the bad times, the times when they had tried to force her off her property. She spoke of estate agents speculators and dubious business people playing dirty tricks, all of whom had queued outside her house over the years, just to receive rebuff over rebuff.

One day, you old hag, your fate will come and get the better of you. I will be waiting for you; it can't be too long now, a very disappointed property tycoon had once said.

"Well, this man has been lying under a marble slab for a long time now. There are quite a few that I have outlived over the years."

She shrugged and smiled.

She also told him that she had never been lucky enough to start her own family, for when she was young or old enough to be married, whichever way you looked at it, most of the young men had wandered off, preferring the modern lifestyle. She had remained without a husband or children until she'd got to an age where the question of starting a family was no longer up for discussion anyway.

"Well, my dear child…" the old lady mumbled, and one could detect a shimmer in her eyes—one of those shimmers that appeared when tears started welling up. "If I am really honest, at times it pains me to be alone. All my friends have gone now. They are already looking down on me. And the young ones, well, none of the young care about a little old lady like me."

She managed to stop her trail of thought before it sent her into melancholy. "But never mind all that now." She shook her head as if to shake off the upcoming sadness. "I don't want to spoil the day for us, and I must tell you how pleased I am to have some company again."

The shuttle shot through the warp one last time. All the wool was used up. The weaver woman reached for the scissors and cut off the overhanging thread. The boy knotted the ends to stop the cloth from fraying. They deposited the bale of cloth on a shelf, took an afternoon snooze, and then, in the late evening, walked through the garden once again. On this round, the old lady asked about the boy's fate.

The boy did not hold back. He spoke about the mean tycoon and his outrageous behaviour. About his father's upset and how it had affected the mood in the whole house, and how he felt that he had to look for a solution to save his poor father and the rest of the family. He spoke about the journey and the difficulties of finding a place for the night.

The old lady rolled her eyes about the latter.

"Sadly, this is how people are these days. The closer you come to town, the colder you will find the hearts."

This in turn caused the boy to admit that as much as he loved being with his host, he would have to continue his journey very soon. And even though he was not quite sure of where to go, and how to go about it, he was on a mission to save his family and needed to continue.

The odd couple sat and chatted until dusk, exactly

to the point where the nightwatchman rang his bell, and the street lanterns shone their yellow light onto the cobblestones of the pavements like a row of pearls.

On this night, it didn't take long for the little boy to drift off to sleep, the cat by his side. Only the little old lady lay awake in her room, staring at the ceiling.

What is going to happen to the boy? she thought. *The world is such a big and dangerous place. And he wants to save his family. But how? With a bag of apples and his walking cane?*

She thought long and hard about what she could give him to help him on his way. A good word, a few apples and some coins from her savings. Those things were obvious, but they would soon be used up. And then what? It became clear to her that he needed more of a long-lasting contribution. Something big. Something for life. Something he could carry with him wherever he went.

She carried on thinking and looking back at her life, weighing up everything she had ever found useful and dismissing all the things that had caused her grief. And as she pondered over the solution, one thing became clearer and clearer. It seemed to be everywhere and anywhere. Something so obvious, yet something we all take for granted.

The cornerstone of a happy life.

That is it, she thought. *That is what I am going to do. That is exactly what the boy needs.*

Happy with herself, she turned over and finally closed her eyes. And as she drifted off into a deep sleep, a smile played across her lips.

The suburb had turned quiet, the lights had been extinguished one by one. The pubs had called last orders and even the last guests finally heard their beds calling. Doors were locked, gates were bolted, and neither man nor beast was to be seen.

All seemed quiet, until there was a sudden loud clatter, almost like hooves thundering on the road. It came from the south, from the wide valley and it approached at speed, gradually getting closer and closer.

A Landauer with its hood up appeared out of the darkness, two black stallions in front, a servant clutching the reins. Weary from the long journey, it took all his concentration to keep the coach on the road. Not far to go now, just a little farther into the town centre, past the cathedral covered in scaffolding, and then towards the villas and manor houses where the rich and the powerful lived.

The yellow glow of the streetlights beamed through the coach window and shone onto a round, gold case lying on the seat.

A hand appeared and the case opened.

A match was struck, a fat cigar lit, and grey smoke rose to the ceiling past a big, fat, round bald head wearing a disproportionately small top-hat.

Finally! Deal done! I have got those yokels firmly in my hand, the head thought.

More smoke rose to the ceiling.

This will be the business deal of my life. I know exactly what to do. And for those two or three awkward farmers who remain, a solution will quickly be found. And then the whole valley is mine.

A nasty smirk presented itself on the tycoon's face. That nasty, that the butler experienced a shiver running down his spine and it felt as if the two horses suddenly accelerated, as if the devil was driving them on. Our two friends in the little house with the wrought-iron turtle doves on the gable had no idea what was going on outside.

That's because sometimes in life, it is better not to have knowledge of all the bad things going on in the world, otherwise we would be far too scared to put one foot in front of the other. On top of that, I saw it as my duty to keep the worries away from the little boy. This is why I did not mention any of this to him the next morning as he eagerly jumped out of bed to embrace the day.

"Come, I want to show you something," the old lady said. "But this time, let us sit on the bench in front of the house, so we don't miss any of the spectacle I want you to witness."

The boy had fed the last bucket of pellets to the sheep and then followed the old lady to the bench. The air was fresh and clean, and the road was empty, apart from a cat heading home from a night's hunting, and a cockerel that crowed his morning call in the distance. The boy and the little old lady were the only people around. After a few minutes, the boy asked impatiently, "What is it you wanted to show me?"

The old weaver woman pointed her head in direction of the road without averting her eyes, sighed quietly but deeply, and then she spoke:

"Look at the people. Watch them and you will learn

everything you ever need to know in life."

And then, suddenly, as if someone had rung an invisible bell, the suburb sprang into action. There was a sudden buzz, almost like when a beehive comes to life as it is met by the morning sun. Curtains opened and behind the glass, sleepy figures stumbled from one room to another. A head with a night cap here and a head with a laced sleeping cap there. Scraps of conversations and upcoming arguments could be heard. *Did you iron my shirt? And where is my waistcoat? You had better hurry up!*

A woman could be heard scolding her husband for staying in the pub all night. The man told his wife that he would rather spend his time with his mates playing cards than listening to her nagging.

In the meantime, the usual hectic morning ritual had spread to every corner of the suburb, into every house and the little boy watched and listened in amazement. Wherever you looked and listened, there was anger, and ill feelings. Everyone seemed to be rushing around in a bad mood. In the meantime a few of the residents had already arrived at the street corner, where a tram left for the city every half hour.

There they stood, dark shadows under their eyes, present in body but not in mind, most of them sucking nervously on a cigarette breakfast.

Some scanned the headlines of the local newspaper, searching for the latest gossip and sensations, no one was speaking a word nor were they acknowledging each other. The tram arrived, quickly filled up with unhappy passengers and then disappeared into the distance. The second group started to gather shortly afterwards. And this carried on and on until the suburb emptied, and silence returned.

The boy was eager to learn what the weaver woman had to say about all of this, but the old lady never said a word. They both continued with their daily chores—checking on the sheep, walking through the meadow, taking lunch and the usual lunchtime nap before working on the loom.

But just before dinner, the old lady insisted that they would take up their seats on the bench in front of the house again. The happenings of the morning seem to repeat themselves, only this time, in reverse order.

The army of workers returned home from their offices and factories. For the boy, watching them intently, they seemed lifeless and depressed, with tired eyes and empty heads, even more so than in the morning. Some disappeared straight into their houses, others were heading to the pubs.

Day after day, the two of them sat on the bench, people watching. Watching how the queues rushed to work and dragged themselves home. And not to forget those who queued patiently at the apothecary to find relief from the aches and pains of the daily grind. There also seemed to be a handful of people no longer of use in the working environment. Worn out and not needed, they sat by their windows peeking through the curtains, lonely and bored.

The boy had seen what he was supposed to see but didn't quite understand the importance of his observations until a couple of days later, when the old lady revealed the secret.

Sitting at the loom, with the shuttle in her hands, she suddenly asked, "Did you see how others went about their day?"

"Yes, I did," answered the boy in anticipation of what was to come.

"Did you notice how tired and worn out they looked, no matter what time of day?"

"Yes."

"Did you also see the long queues outside the apothecary, and notice those who have worked hard all their life and are now surplus to requirements?"

"Yes, weaver woman, that I have seen."

"Well, it cannot be any different," she said. "It is almost as if one would break a piece off oneself every day and burn it until there's nothing left to burn."

The boy nodded.

"Most humans follow their false beliefs to such an extent that they waste their most precious attributes, and they do not seem to stop, ever. Not even when the clock strikes twelve. Thus, I want you to do things differently. Look after yourself and keep yourself safe. The most precious commodity in life is your health."

Suddenly, the room filled with sunlight and the boy could see everything very clearly.

Health, he thought. *We don't miss it until we have too little of it.*

"Health," he repeated aloud.

What a powerful word, thought the little old lady.

Especially coming from a child's mouth.

"I suppose your next question now will be how to look after your health?"

She turned towards the boy and took a full shuttle out of his hand.

"I am not as rich as all the entrepreneurs and tycoons, nor am I as famous as an opera singer, but there is one thing I have been all my life, and that is healthy. In fact, I have been healthier than anybody I have ever come across. And all due to the five free gifts nature has to offer. Today, you and I have already enjoyed plenty of them."

She took her hand and counted them off on her fingers. Once again, her voice broke into a sing song, as if she recited a poem.

"Fresh air to fill your lungs, fresh water to quench your thirst and to refresh your body, fresh food to keep your strength, daily exercise to sharpen the mind, and a good night's rest."

He had to smile as he reminisced about the day. The fresh air streaming through the bedroom window and sucked deep into his lungs. Sweet air coming up from the meadow, from the flowers and trees. The water, the little creek leading from the spring, the food he had grown from Mother Earth with his own bare hands, the daily walks with the little old lady, and the soft cosy bed to rest in at the end of the night.

"Health is my most important treasure," he said, and looked towards the window.

The old lady was sure that her guest had understood his lesson, and she knew that there was nothing more she could do. She had to let him go, even though she loathed being on her own again. But she also knew that health would not be enough to cross the plans of the tycoon. Something was constantly running away, something the little boy needed to be able to overcome if he wanted to achieve his goal.

And because of this, the little old lady, acting on a hunch, sent the boy to learn about the origin of time.

CHAPTER 4

Time

...is your ally. Treat it accordingly

I could feel the weight on the boy's shoulders. Not because he had slung his cane and his little bundle of provisions over them, but because the town seemed to suffocate him. Earlier that morning, he had bid farewell to the little old weaver woman and the two cast-iron turtle doves on the roof. He had entered the street with a lot of gusto and followed the directions he had memorised in his head for the second stage of his journey, heading to a place where more of life's lessons awaited him.

With all his senses bursting, he was on the lookout for the orientation points the weaver woman had given him: the turning point for all the coaches which also served as a stop for the tram; the magnificent mall with its triumphal arch; and a little further down, the merchant houses, only noticeable because the old town wall formed an almost natural barrier around them. Over the years, the weather had eroded the stone and really and truly, unless you had a very keen eye, it was only the old town gate and the two watch towers that made this ancient town wall noticeable at all. Behind it, one seemingly entered a different world; huge palaces made from steel and glass.

Build next to each other, there were rows and rows of them, like carrots in a field. For the boy, watching the sun creating sparkles on the glass facades, it certainly looked like a magical place. And before he even noticed it, he had lost the last waypoint and I nearly lost him.

Apart from the sights and sounds, there was also a plethora of unfamiliar smells for the nose and a constant rumble, as if the world were coming to an end. I won't even try to explain the smells, but pleasant they were definitely not. The very moment one succumbed to the sweet smell of something nice, a stench came rising from a gutter where rubbish had been carelessly thrown on the road, or even from an open sewer.

And the people.

The people were just racing about, each to their own, pushing and shoving, shouting and screaming.

One thing was obvious: the rule of compassion did not apply here at all. And so it happened that some careless man pushed our little boy to one side, only for the poor child to fall to the floor with his arms stretched out wide.

"Be careful, child," the ruffian hissed at him. Followed by, "Out of the way, you nuisance – get out of the way!"

The little bundle smashed to the floor. The knotted

edges opened and spilled the contents onto the cobbled street. Half a dozen apples, freshly harvested from the old lady's apple tree, rolled in between the legs of the other pedestrians. As soon as the boy went to grab one, a large boot had turned it into mush. The other apples suffered the same fate.

It wasn't long before all his possessions were lost in the crowd. Ruined! *Everything* was ruined, including the soft linen shirt the old lady had woven for him. It was dirty and torn. Everything seemed pointless, pointless to try and save what clearly could not be saved.

And even worse, there it was again, the ugly fat toad, croaking away loudly. The fear the boy felt, whilst in midst of this pushing and shoving mass, had summoned the toad to the occasion.

I called over to the boy.

"Put your hands on your head and quickly dash out of there, sideways if you can.

"Quickly, before they drag you further down and stamp you into the ground."

The poor child jumped up, only to crash into someone's hip, but then he finally managed to push past them, using all his strength. His little hands tried to protect his head from anything that could harm him—from briefcases and handbags and all the other stuff adults usually carried around.

He fell to the floor one more time before managing to break free. He made it into a side lane, and there he came to rest, shaking and with wobbly knees.

"My things," he sighed. "I have nothing left and no

idea where I am."

A big tear rolled down his little face.

I too was searching for some encouraging words and needless to say, it took a while before I was able to speak.

"Yes, you may have lost more than you had when you started your journey, but look, at least you managed to get out of the crowd alive and you have successfully preserved your biggest asset."

The boy dusted himself off.

First his head, then his shoulders, and finally, his legs. You could see a hint of blue and purple on parts of his body where bruises tried to mark this last adventure, but he was in one piece.

"Take it as a lesson not to deviate from your intended path," I said to him. "Do not be blinded by sparkle and glow you come across."

We continued our journey and started looking for the cuckoo clock said to mark the entrance of the origin of time. We passed a parade of shops on the way. In one of the windows a display of colourful handmade sweets and glazed pastries was temptingly displayed, and behind it, some well-to-do customers. Elegantly clothed, their children donning the latest fashion. The boy, hungry after all the exhaustions, stopped and pressed his nose against the window. And of course, it didn't take long until he got a response.

"Hey you! Yes, you. Strays are not welcome here. Off! Off you go. And a bit sharpish," the shopkeeper shouted. The boy got a terrible fright. Accompanied by the mocking comments of the well-to-do, he ran further down the lane.

And once again, thick blobs of tears cascaded down his face.

What was this place? This was nothing like the friendly little community he had grown up in, in his valley by the mountains. His heart and lungs were already pounding as he turned the corner into the next lane, where he was confronted and growled at by an enormous, aggressive guard dog baring its teeth. He managed to get himself to a little flower bed. More stumbling than walking by now, he summoned his last strength, jumped across and let himself fall onto the little patch of green adjacent to it. Curled up like a little hedgehog, he started to cry. Never, ever had I seen a little child cry so much.

I was lost for words and would have loved to have comforted him in my arms, but that was not possible. I stared at the little creature and summoned my friends, thinking they may help him.

First, I called *Hope*, but she didn't answer, then I called *Love*, but she also remained silent.

My last option was to ask for *Luck*.

"If we could only have a little bit of luck here," I begged, eyes peering up at the sky.

Grey clouds started appearing. They were hanging deep, and it seemed as if they were pushing each other, getting bigger and heavier all the time. It looked as if it was going to rain, a summer storm coming down on the hot, sweaty town. But then, all of a sudden, a touch of blue appeared, a ray of sunshine gleaming through the dark skies. Luck had begun its journey and landed exactly at the boy's feet. The sunshine shone brightly into his face, and his crying got less and less. And then we could hear it! There it was.

"Cuckoo… Cuckoo."

I turned around. *Wasn't that…?*

And again.

"Cuckoo… Cuckoo."

Oh yes! The cuckoo clock. The origin of…

"Time. Come on, boy, it's time!" I shouted. "It's here, somewhere, not far away.

"Come on. Up! Up!"

We raced through the lanes towards the calling bird, turning off into the direction from which we thought the call had come. And there it was. We stood in front of a machine the size of a man. The iron bird had just made its last call and was about to slide back into its bird house. It was five past twelve, not only by the standards of time but also by the wobbly legs of the poor boy. So, I said to him, "Look, can you see the old rusty sign above the door: *To the Origin of time*? Knock! Knock before the rain starts. It's already starting to drizzle. We don't want to get soaked today as well."

I didn't have to say it a second time. The boy knocked on the door. It was a confident knock and not long after, an old man in a white work coat with a magnifying glass wedged between one eye opened the door.

"Who sent you?"

"The weaver woman."

The skinny, overly tall man pushed his fists into his sides and bent over, first forwards, then backwards, arching into a horseshoe shape. You could hear his old bones crack and creak as he straightened himself out again.

"I haven't heard from her in a long time, but of course, do come in and tell me what this is all about," he said in a voice not quite befitting an old man.

"And while you are here, I have a couple of things you can help me with. My back is letting me down these days. Again…"

The man seemed friendly enough, and for the second time in his life, the boy entered into the house of a stranger. And what a house it was. Walls, floors, tables and shelf tops—everything was covered with clocks or parts thereof. Due to the enormous variations of clocks, the constant, but conflicting levels of 'tick tock' sounds created a hectic feel around the place, which was occasionally interrupted by a chime or a bird song. It was all a bit confusing for the little boy. He was not used to so much noise, nor did he know where to put his eyes, and it so happened that he stumbled over a timepiece lying on the floor and crashed straight into the old man's behind.

"Mind yourself," the old man said. "I know the place is screaming for a tidy-up and it would have long been done had it not been for my masterpiece which calls for my utmost attention."

The smile crossing the old man's lips indicated to me that working on the masterpiece seemed to be most enjoyable and not much of a chore to him. A bit like tending to a difficult lover.

To give into the boy's curiosity, he turned the walk towards his workshop into a guided tour through time, explaining the difference between a bracket clock and a grandfather clock, why a wall clock needed a spring mechanism, and the purpose of a balance wheel.

Strange words were passing the old man's lips. Difficult to understand, but important enough to help one navigate one's way through all the springs, coils, screws and cones.

"As you can see, I am a clockmaker," he said as he opened the door to his workshop.

Behind the door was a huge hall, with floor-length windows on both sides. The summer storm was now raging at full force, with rain hammering hard against the glass, that loud that it drowned out the *ticking* and the *tocking* coming from adjacent rooms. It smelled of oil and glue and metal shavings. A dozen lamps lit the big hall. They shone their light on the floor and over to the corner where the workbench and lathe were set up. On the wall above, an array of tools, sorted by size and nature. Screwdrivers, files, drills, compasses and many other tools whose correct names would only have been known to a clockmaker. Below the worktop, and to the left of the lathe, a line of cupboards filled to the brim.

"This is where I keep everything," he said. "The clock cases as well as the tiniest gear wheels."

"And down there, in that corner below the linen cloth?" asked the boy. "What is down there?"

"Oh, yes, I nearly forgot to mention the most important thing of all," answered the clockmaker.

The rain was now accompanied by thunder and lightning, the enormous flashes crashing to the floor. The centre of the storm was right above the town, and the water had won over the sealed ground and gushed along the gutter. At first it had been small streams, and then wide rivers taking up half of the thoroughfare. Not a soul could be seen out and about. Carelessly discarded rubbish was washing down the road.

The little boy did not notice any of this. He had fixed his attention to the box lying on the floor, hidden under another linen cloth.

It cannot be a clock, he thought. *It's impossible that this is a clock. It is far too big.*

From the centre of the cloth, a rope led to the ceiling and fed around a wheel hanging from a strong crossbeam, only to reappear on the other side. A winch.

The clockmaker pulled on the rope and hoisted the cover into the air. Thousands of little dust particles flew through the room and tickled the boy's nose, making him sneeze. As he looked up again, he saw the most peculiar machine he had ever set eyes on.

"Here she is," the clockmaker cried out in a tone of excitement and pride. "The clock of all clocks."

Oh, it is a clock, thought the boy.

"A church clock. That's what you would call it. I've been working on it most of my life."

The expressions on the man's face seemed to change. He spoke about the origin of time and when mankind had begun to measure it. He spoke about the old belief that something was only real if it could be measured, and about the attempts to utilise the sunlight, the moon and the stars, and also the Milky Way to navigate.

How it wasn't until much later before they started

using gravity to read time by the means of falling sand grains or water drops, at least until that day when someone had extracted ore from deep in the ground, made it glow and shaped it to his desire.

The birth of iron, and with it, countless means of construction. And of course it could also be used for the manufacturing of clocks. He spoke of the many times he had disassembled this clock and put it back together in a different fashion. He had changed the gear wheels, coils, pins, nuts and bolts, always in search of perfection, until he lost track of what he had already tried and what not. Over and over again, hundreds, if not thousands of times. "They call it an obsession," he said. "But let them. They have all tried and all have failed."

Suddenly, the old man fell silent. He looked up. Was he even still talking to the boy or more to himself?

The boy felt the irritation and asked, "What did all the others try?" and after a little pause, "and what did they fail at?"

"I will try and explain it to you, child," said the man, and stared at his machine once again. "What I want more than anything, ever since I first made a clock hand move. Well…"

The thunder drowned out the rest of his words.

"I am creating the most elegant, the most precise, the most robust, and dare I say it myself; the most beautiful clockwork one can imagine. And I am building it for the highest tower in town, where it can be seen from far afield. I am creating this for all eternity, just as all the other monuments mankind has ever created are for eternity."

The thunder had stopped, the rain slowed down, and the boy stood with his mouth wide open.

He was astonished, almost as if someone had opened a door to another world. The clockmaker seemed to find contentment just looking at his masterpiece. He stroked the frame, and then from above he felt for the anchor wheel, turning it until they both heard a loud *click*. Next he pushed the anchor down and lifted the crown wheel. Another *click*.

For me, the whole matter did indeed look a bit like an obsession, and I was sure the boy thought the same. But before I could even gather my thoughts, something began to move in the heart of the clock. Hard to notice with all those wheels and coils, but one part seemed to set the next into motion.

"Watch it," spoke the obsessed man.

"Watch what?" asked the boy.

"The *clicking* and the *clocking*, the *ticking* and the *tocking*. How the machine springs to life, as if the hands of a ghost are moving it."

The wheels, big and small, turned so smoothly as if they were in unison. Coils, spirals and tractions stretched and pulled themselves playfully together. The pendulum at the back of the box swung majestically through the air and motioned the second hand, to which its shaft was attached. I rubbed my eyes in disbelief. Indeed, I stood in front of a...

"Masterpiece," the clockmaker said. "That is what mankind will call it."

He moved a little lever.

"Genius, they will call me, and soon forget the names they used to call me before."

The little boy had long ceased to understand.

And frankly, so had I.

"You may look bewildered, child, but you have just been witnessing the fact that I am about to complete my life's work. It is even more elegant, robust, precise and magnificent than I dared to imagine."

The watchmaker stamped his feet for joy, clapped his hands in excitement and even whistled a happy tune, so joyous that the little boy joined into the celebrations and the two forgot everything around them. At least, until the clockmaker's aging lungs put a stop to it. He leaned back into the workings, disengaged the anchor by pushing it down, and the whole thing stopped.

"There's only a couple more things to do," he said, breathlessly. "Just a few. Work for a healthy back. Will you help me?"

For the next few days, dark clouds continued to dominate the sky. On top of that, a strong north-easterly wind brought a chill to the town, normally only known in autumn. And just like the hospitality of the clockmaker, which was second to none, it was another reason for everyone to remain in the house.

The table was laden, a comfy bed was waiting behind the workshop, and the invitation to be a part of something magnificent, all of this, needless to say, meant that the boy was happy and content.

The clockmaker too. First of all he had company, and secondly—and much more important to him even though he tried to disguise the fact—he was at last able to carry out the remaining work to the clock. He knew the clockwork mechanism like the back of his hand. Which parts went where, their functions, the distribution of the transition, the resistances.

He had calculated it over and over again, that often that he knew the figures off by heart. There was not the slightest doubt. The construction was perfect. He had put his whole heart into this machine, at least as long as his aging body let him. But now, his back was hunched, his fingers shaky, and his eyesight weak.

But he wouldn't have been the best of his kind if he hadn't found a solution for this too. A magnifying glass for his weak eyes. Leather strapping to hold his fingers still. And for the bad back?

For that, he had the boy.

"It needs to be in the right place."

"Here?"

"No, further to the left."

"Here?"

"Yes, good; you can put it right there."

The boy had quickly learned to handle the oil can. The instructions were clear. He was only allowed to place one drop into the pivot hole. No more, no less. That would be enough to keep the clockwork running for years to come.

So, there he was, sometimes on his back, sometimes on his belly, crawling through the clockwork, wherever the directions from the clockmaker sent him. Next, the screws. They must not be loose. That would disturb the smooth running of the wheels.

"Another turn?"

"No, just a half-turn. Be gentle, child."

"It won't turn any further."

"Good, can you see the one above it, to your left?"

"Yes."

"Let's do that next."

They both worked until late into the night. And the next day and the morning after that. They only had one brief interruption when a lady came by to show an interest in a grandfather clock, which in turn gave the boy chance to question the clockmaker about something that had been playing on his mind.

What plans had he made for his masterpiece once it was finished? This was the question the little boy needed to ask. The clockmaker explained that in his eyes, there was only one worthy place for his clock. The cathedral, the gigantic building made from hewn sandstone and marble, situated in the centre of the town.

Renovations had been taking place for many years to save the crumbling building from further deterioration. It had already received vast donations and there was no end in sight. The expectations of the cardinal were just as high as his desire for a place in front of God.

Only the best and the magnificent should have a place in God's house, and at the same time, be earth-inspiring to entice future visitors. He also had a good understanding of how to squeeze the last shilling out of his flock. And this he had also tried with our friend the clockmaker, whose efforts to build a masterpiece had gotten about and eventually reached the cardinal. A construction that would fit effortlessly into the clock tower. Yes, that would be it.

"And then this madman suggested in all earnest, that I should donate my masterpiece to the church. For free. As absolution for my sins," said the clockmaker with a bitter voice.

His top lip started trembling and I could see that the old man was trying hard to compose himself.

"Well, I am not the most innocent angel under the sky, and I have not always believed. And I am aware that my masterpiece can only be installed on the highest point of the cathedral, the clock tower, but at the same time, I want to retire soon. And to do so, I need reasonable compensation for my work. But the cardinal refused."

I felt a bit sorry for the old clockmaker as he stood there, his hands dangling down his sides, staring out the window for quite a while.

There was no tool to fix his problem. No file, no oil can, and no compass could help him solve the matter. *It will gather dust in my workshop instead,* thought the clockmaker despondent. *And so will I if I have to.*

"But there must be another way," answered the little boy.

"I don't know," mumbled the clockmaker. "I really don't know."

The old man was not prepared to give up. There was always hope, thus, he avoided the boy's comments. Instead, he asked about the boy's fate. His home, his family and his reason for leaving. And what he heard brought back memories to long forgotten times.

That squeaking baldie is at it again, he thought. *Found himself a new victim. If that is the case, the farming folk in the valley don't stand a chance. The boy doesn't stand a chance either. Not only is he mean—this fat, round face under the far too small top hat—but he is also shrewd and devious.*

The old man's thoughts returned to the time when there had been more than a dozen clockmakers in town, when he himself was in the prime of his life, no hunched back, no leather straps to hold his hands in place. It was at that time when large factories popped out of the ground like mushrooms, presenting their owners with enormous riches.

The tycoon had opened a factory for precision mechanisms and plenty of the little independent workshops had gone out of business because of it. Only very few survived, either by repairing clocks or by creating and manufacturing bespoke timepieces for the rich and famous.

But the tycoon could not get enough.

Next, he turned his mind towards the sheep farmers, and soon enough, he had destroyed all the weavers' little workshops in the very same manner.

What was left were empty houses and overgrowing meadows, immediately turned into more smoking chimneys and glass palaces. And from then on, everything the tycoon turned his hand to, became a success. And the more people suffered at his hand, the richer he became. The profits he made paved the path to what he really wanted, power and control.

"To preserve all that is dear to my heart, I need to

look after my health first," said the boy.

"And I know how to do that, but the weaver woman has told me that I will need to have many other gifts before I can realise my plans."

The clockmaker had stopped what he was working on and cleared his throat. Not because he had something to say, but because he felt a lump in it.

"I also have a friend with me. He helps me with my battles against the toad," the boy said.

The man cleared his throat for the second time.

"To the devil with it," he said aloud.

The boy crossed his arms in front of his chest and looked bewildered at him. The clockmaker fixed his eyes on him in a very adamant sort of way.

Pity has never helped anybody, he thought. *It only exacerbates the problem. We need to help the boy to help himself.*

"Wait here, I need to think," he mumbled, and left the workshop without another word. On his return, he took off his work apron and placed it on the floor. He asked the boy to sit next to it.

"The old lady sent you to me for a reason," he said with stern words. "Thus, I will give you the essence of the second treasure of life that we all own. Can you think what it may be?"

He unfolded a small piece of paper.

Time. It heals all pain, and it takes all sorrow. It lingers in love and yet presents us with the end of our lives.

"Now, listen child," said the clockmaker. "There is much more to this than meets the eye."

He spoke about the sorrows in the valley, about the strains and dangers that every journey brought.

About how being homesick was much more painful than bruises and scratches, and how even the worst pain one had ever experienced would be healed eventually through time.

"Time heals. You just have to let it do its work," he said to the little boy.

"And then there is love," continued the man. "Just when you think that time is flying by, you spend it with someone you love, and it seems to slow down."

Outside, the wind had stopped blowing and blue patches could once again be seen in the sky.

Sunshine flooded through the windows and reflected in the face of the tower clock.

"Every phase in your life will have a purpose," the clockmaker remarked. "Time will always heal and let you forget the bad things. But time can also be found in the good things, in love, in luck. But nothing will be forever.

"And just so we don't forget, time has also given us the end. In time, we will all have to die. Mortality is the other big gift, right next to life. It just makes everything we live for so much better."

The clockmaker folded the little note up and felt the warm summer sunshine warming up his back.

"I will keep an eye on time," said the little boy.

"You will have to."

"It will be precious to me."

"That it will."

The clockmaker pressed the little note into the boy's

palm and winked at him.

"If only I could read," said the boy all of a sudden. "Where I come from, the…"

The clockmaker lifted his hand, got up and dusted himself off. Then he put his fists into his sides and bent himself in horseshoe fashion once again. His rusty bones groaned and creaked. He took the boy by the hand and pulled him towards himself.

"You really don't know how to read and write?"

The boy shook his head.

"Then it is about time you get to your next destination."

"My next destination?" asked the boy, bewildered.

"Yes," answered the clockmaker. "It is about time. I will send you to the place of knowledge."

CHAPTER 5

Society

Take a good look around and never give up

Shortly after the tycoon had made his first appearance in the valley, a convoy of trucks had arrived, loaded to the brim with building materials. A camp was due to be erected on one of the fields the tycoon had bought from an old farmer, a single man worn out from all the years of hard work looking after his land, and now longing for a quieter life.

The deal was struck in no time at all. More than fifty gold sovereigns had changed hands, quite a mind-boggling sum, much discussed amongst those who hung on to watch the upcoming developments. Blinded by the sparkling sovereigns, the old farmer had saddled his horse and left the very same day, never to be seen again.

The new arrivals busying themselves, were watched

closely.

They had brought heavy trek oxen, tents, rations, and carts full of all sorts of materials, including sawn planks, beams, sheets of wood, window glass, iron fittings, lime, and a vast selection of different tools.

They did not waste time starting their mission.

First, they tore down the old farmhouse together with its adjacent barn, felled all the beautiful old fruit trees, and then dug a big hole in the ground. They mixed clay with lime and started to fire bricks. Next, they raised the ground floor of the building to head height, leaving gaps for windows and doors on all sides. Oak beams were set into place above the building, and not long afterwards, the first interior walls went up. The building grew and grew, causing the local residents to wonder about the purpose of all of this, but no one found the answer.

"The largest cart needs to go back into town. Take four horses," the foreman said to the carpenter. "We need more beams."

Both men turned to the drawing. Behind them, an army of workers that did not rest.

"This is where the windmill will be." The foreman pointed a finger at the plan.

"And the barracks for the men will go here."

"And the water? Where are we going to get water from?" asked the carpenter.

"Just get the well builder to dig another hole in the ground. If that does not succeed and it means taking water from the farmers, so be it. As long as we stick to our timetable, I don't care."

The foreman was used to not faffing around. His customer was demanding. It was his job to get the warehouse and all its outbuildings completed in time. A trading post so to speak, where all the goods produced in the valley would later be weighed and packaged before being transported into town.

"Tell your men that a barrel of rum will be waiting for them if the roof is on by tomorrow."

The carpenter raised his eyebrows and tightened his lips. *That will be difficult to achieve,* he thought.

"And some silver coins for yourself," the foreman said.

"Of course, boss," the carpenter said, suddenly convinced, and rubbed his hands.

"You know you can rely on me."

The wind, this time coming from the mountains in the south, picked up and as it blew into the valley it pushed the clouds away. They soon disappeared and the sky above the valley turned bright blue, usually a sign for a few mild days ahead and little rain, and a great help to the strangers getting their work done. That would certainly please the tycoon. Everything was going to plan.

The boy and I had no idea what was going on in the valley for we were busy finding our way about town, ready for our next chapter. Every step we took led us deeper and deeper into the town centre. One lane looked just like the next. The clockmaker had told the boy to follow the sun. He was to take exactly 5.000 steps and his goal would be right in front of him.

There were masses of people about, just like the day

when we first arrived in town almost a week ago. There were different kinds of people, split into four groups. Firstly, there were the well-to-do men and women, easily marked out by their attire and the way they walked. They did not rush, they strolled along the lanes and boulevards. Their minds were set to gather material wealth, and when they had amassed enough, they turned to entertainment. But no matter how glamorous they looked, their eyes looked cold and lethargic. So, their desire to achieve at all costs and at all times did not contribute to their happiness and effectively had no meaning.

The second group consisted of the workers. They all seemed to use the same tailor, that's how uniform they looked. Dark trousers, grey shirt, black waistcoat, and a felt hat with a wide brim, hat band and a pinched middle. You could only tell them apart if you looked at their figures. Some were tall and thin; others plump and short. Some carried their briefcase in their left hand, others in their right. They came from the suburbs and raced along the lanes taking long steps. Every inch of their bodies seemed agitated. They had important tasks to carry out, and if everything went to plan, then one day they may also be elevated into the class of the well-to-do, to a group that spend its time on meaningless matters and easily got bored.

The largest group by far was the third one, including labourers, servants, maids and coachmen, and all others whose job it was to keep the town alive. Suddenly, someone shouted from behind us. "Careful, horse droppings!"

The boy managed to jump aside. Only just.

"Thank you," he said.

"Pleasure," said the smiling road sweeper, before he set his broom to work on the offending article, all the time followed by the dismissive eyes of a lady watching from the window, wearing a sparkling ruby on her finger and a thick gold chain around her neck.

"Oh dear, I am so sorry," sighed a maid after she knocked her heavy shopping basket into the boy's side. But before he could even acknowledge her, he could hear a voice barking, "Where on earth have you been?" The voice belonged to the maid's master, who stood waiting for her. The frightened maid ran towards him, ignoring the little boy.

Having observed the appalling manners of these 'fine' people, I shook my head. It was as if the third group of people and their existence was only tolerated as long as they had their use. We left the theatre of pretence behind us and carried on walking, nearly overlooking the fourth and final group in this town: the beggars, the cripples, and the vagabonds, those who were broken, ignored and despised—all those who lived in poverty, people who were pitied by the third group, ignored by the workers and scorned by the well-to-do.

They led a life of misery, some curled up in a sheltered corner, others holding out their hands for a spare penny—a hand that often remained empty just like the hearts of those passing. At the end of the lane, two young tearaways had set up a shoe-cleaning station, a boy and a girl, brother and sister by the looks of it. Their clothes had not seen a bar of soap for quite some time, nor had their little faces.

"Clean shoes, clean shoes," they called.

"Clean shoes, for a penny."

The pair had only just started to gain the attention of the passing public when a policeman stormed towards them. With a truncheon in his right hand and his whistle in the left, it looked as if he was going to start the fight of a lifetime.

"Vermin," he screamed. "Away with you or I will drag you off by the ears."

The pair disappeared in the blink of an eye. A David without his slingshot was no opponent for Goliath. Suddenly, the policeman noticed the little boy, and the upcoming glare in his eyes and his twitching lips made it perfectly clear in which group he put him.

With the whistle and his angry screams still ringing in our ears, we ran as fast as we could and hid behind a well. We were very lucky that we got away.

It seemed as if the policeman wasn't that eager to chase us after all. Order had been restored plus his shift was nearly over, his rumbling belly requiring its lunchtime beverage. Thankfully, he stuck the truncheon back into his belt and walked proudly back to the police station.

By now, the sun stood high in the sky and hot air hovered above the cobblestones. The boy quenched his thirst from the well.

"Let us take a break," I said.

He showed no reaction.

At first, I thought he had spilled some water on his little cheeks, maybe because of the searing midday heat. But I was wrong. "The weaver woman was right," said the boy. "The closer you get to the town, the colder the hearts."

He stopped and looked at me.

"I don't want to stay here, Courage," he said.

There was nothing teary about his voice. It was just a little bit deeper than normal. It sounded like a voice of someone who had suddenly realised that the journey he had embarked upon was a lot more difficult than it had first seemed. The little boy looked up to the sky and his thoughts embarked on a long journey, away from the lanes of the strange town, past the cuckoo clock and the cast iron turtle doves, and then across the thin, dry meadows towards the mountains and the clearing where the old oak tree stood. Over to the lush meadows, the clear creeks and where the air smelled sweet, to the place the little boy held so dear in his heart.

I wonder what they are doing right now? he asked himself. *Wonder if my little brother is still crawling into the linen cupboard to play hide and seek.*

It wouldn't usually take long before he couldn't help himself giggling, a sign for his two sisters to start looking for him, the master of disguise. And even though his sisters already knew where the little boy had hidden, they pretended to look for him until the little cutie could no longer contain his excitement. When the doors would fly wide open, and they would pull him out of the cupboard and tickle his little feet.

Mother would be sitting in the lounge, knitting a winter jumper for the little one, a smile on her face that only a loving mother could have.

Father would still be working the fields. Even more

so in the midst of the summer, there was plenty to get on with. But he would always be home when the sun set, sitting side by side with his wife, watching his children with his kind eyes, children who very much reminded him of himself, and if God agreed, they would grow up to be like him.

"I want to go home," said the boy. "Just home."

I had heard this tune quite often. People being homesick. This usually happened for fear of the unknown. It had been happening for thousands of years, since the beginning of mankind. I was well aware of all the excuses, all the reasons why one should return to what one was used to, the things that seemed safe. And there were vast numbers of people who did go back home. People, whom I, Courage, had failed.

"Can you hear the toad, boy?" I said. "You are now calling it yourself."

No answer.

"I want to be honest with you," I continued. I took my time with what I wanted to say next, for he was a little boy in a big wide world. And the big wide world did not care much about him, but I did.

"We will not return home for a long time yet," I said quietly.

The boy turned his head and looked to the floor. I could see in his eyes how much he missed the love and warmth he had received at home.

He was a bit like a fish out of water.

"The whole world is changing," I said. "Imagine it like an ocean in which you have learned to swim. But the water might dry out and then what, little fish?"

"I don't know," answered the boy.

"See, and this is why we have to find the place the clockmaker has told us about."

By now the toad was croaking as loudly as it could. A noise creating shivers running down one's spine. There it was, heading straight for the little boy, who was still trying to sink into the floor. A relentless moaning was spouting from its mouth, and after each croak it licked its nostrils to take away the secretions. And when it was only a couple of feet away from the little boy, it stood upright and inflated its throat. It's ugly and glibbery looking humps dripping with slime.

"The oak tree, the thin grass," I whispered into the boy's ear. "Do you remember?"

The little body curled up further. His head rested on his knees, his little hands pressing firmly into it, that hard that his knuckles turned white.

"The valley. Your loved ones!"

No reaction.

The toad was licking its lips again.

Then it slowly extended its long tongue, bit by bit, far enough for the tongue to be just an inch away from the boy's head.

I begged him, "The oak, your loved ones. Please, you must remember!"

It was only a matter of time, and the toad would win over the innocent child. Time that would decide the fate of the boy.

"The tycoon," I shouted. "He will destroy everything

you ever hold dear."

"No," shouted the boy and jumped up, "that he will never do."

He hammered his little fists against the wall of the well, and at the same time stomping his feet on the cobble stones as hard as he could. The eyes of the toad widened and as it jumped to keep out the way, it stumbled over its own tongue and fell over backwards. In its panic, it crawled back to where it had come from.

Some of the passers-by had stopped and watched the goings on. They stared at the strange child, how he was relieving his rage by the well. The well-to-do put their noses high up in the air. The workers rushed past, shaking their heads and some of the tradesmen, maids and servants stared at him, full of pity. But I, I had to laugh.

"So, you did remember," I said. "You only have to make a move and the toad disappears."

"Yes, Courage," answered the boy. The blood in his hand pulsed dull and hard. It felt good and he tried to keep the tension for a little longer before he let it leave his body. Then he looked at me with a look of determination that was far from childlike.

"If I need to be a fish out of water, I will learn how to do so. I might even be the first fish to climb a mountain. The first fish ever to cross even the darkest of paths."

I nodded. I was proud of him for overcoming his fear. He had nearly abandoned his journey, and if he had done so, his life would have taken a new direction with no turning back. *And what would I, Courage, be without my little brother, Anger?* I thought.

"Well, my friend, let's go and see where the knowledge lives," I suggested.

"Yes," he answered, stood up and walked towards a building that bore a quill, ink and paper within its crest.

CHAPTER 6

Help

...sometimes comes quite unexpectedly

Isn't it strange how we are always especially susceptible to our own weaknesses just before we are in reach of our goals? How even the smallest aches and pains turn into tortures, agonies? How they suddenly drain us so that we think that we are about to drop dead on the spot. At least, that's how the boy felt as he took his last steps towards the crest. Finally arriving at his next chapter he sat on one of the bollards to rest up.

The building itself was huge, about a hundred feet long and sixty feet wide. It consisted of three storeys covered with a large, hipped roof set with little dormer windows, evenly spaced.

The windows were framed in white, ornately carved frames which gave the otherwise modest-looking building a playful and inviting look.

The arc on the broadside facing the road bore a large crest. The facade had weathered over the years, but on the whole, the yellow building shone brightly in the sunlight. It was not as glamorous as some of the big merchant houses built from red fired bricks surrounding the market square. But it did not have to be glamorous and nor was it intended to be. The merchant houses had been built to demonstrate economic power, wealth expressed through many a hand-carved gargoyle, figurines, and other decorations.

This building, however, had been erected to serve a different purpose. It was designed to harbour lots of children and a handful of adults.

"Come on then," I said to the boy. "Let us go and explore the inside of the school."

"This is a school?" The boy was impressed.

He pushed his body upright to slide off the bollard but then, just as his feet hit the ground, he felt that pain again. But this time it was different—it was so much stronger.

I winked at the boy and pointed at the gate.

"Come," I said.

By then I had asked him for the second time.

The crowd around us had disappeared. Lunch was over, so it seemed, and the well-to-do had filled their bellies and strolled home.

The workers had rushed back to their offices, whilst the labourers, the maids and the servants were looking forward to the end of the day. But for us, the day was only just beginning.

"Stop! Where do you think you are going?" A strict voice barked out, coming from a shielded corner under the arc. The gatekeeper stood firm, his grey uniform almost blending into the darkness of the entrance. There was no way of getting past him.

"Nowhere, it's nothing," mumbled the boy apologetically and hid behind the next corner.

"Come on, boy," I said with my most encouraging voice. "There must be another way of getting in."

We started walking round the building, looking for another entrance, even if it meant an open cellar window. We were adamant that this busybody of a gatekeeper would not stop us. We found a narrow lane to the back of the school, dirty and dark, and in it a pile of wooden crates, formerly used to transport apples and now carelessly thrown aside. Furthermore, the lane was strewn with rotting fruit and vegetables, much to the delight of the town's rats and other vermin.

We followed the lane towards a little corner and, *oh, look who is here!* The two young children with the shoeshine box. They were just as shocked to see the boy as the boy was to see them. Seeing them close up, they looked even scruffier than they had before. But their eyes were pure and innocent and full of sparkle, and suddenly the dark lane did not seem as dark anymore. Seconds later, after all three had overcome their initial shock, the girl grinned.

"Did the copper scare you off?" she asked.

The boy held back.

"Happens to us every day. We just hide until it's safe to come out again."

72

Her brother nodded. He took a piece of wood out of his pocket and started chewing on it.

"I only just managed to get away." The boy winked. He was slowly acclimatising to getting himself away from threatening situations.

"You are not going to give us away, are you?" the little brother asked carefully.

Just that very moment, a mechanical click was to be heard, coming from a window bolt. The children raised their heads to see what was happening. A good ten feet above, at one of the school's windows, a slender hand came into view. It moved a hook into a window eyelet, sank it in and pulled the window open. The hand disappeared and the clatter of stiletto heels on a hard surface sounded from within.

"I have to get up there," said the little boy, pointing at the window.

"What, into the school?" asked the girl. "Don't be daft. It's for the privileged, not for kids like us."

"Well, I'm going anyway," said the little boy, looking sternly into the sceptical eyes of the two young siblings. "Are you going to help me or not?"

The siblings put their heads together and whispered amongst themselves, discussing the strange boy, wondering what he could be up to.

Then they started giggling.

"Of course we will. As long as we stick together, we can master every hurdle", said the little brother. Our boy was astonished at this well-rehearsed sentence but couldn't finish the thought because the girl suddenly took over.

They started stacking the boxes into a wide platform on which they then erected a somewhat wobbly tower. With the boy standing on top, the little brother in the middle and the girl at the bottom, they passed box after box right up to the top until the boy was just short of reaching the window ledge.

The whole thing looked much like the tower of Babel, only far more unstable. The boy continued stacking box on top of box, one after the other, higher and higher until it was not safe to stack any further. Next, he stretched towards the corner of the wall.

Better not make a mistake now, he thought, *otherwise, I am going to end up with broken bones. Best not to even think about falling. And best not to look down either.*

The two siblings had stretched themselves out as far as possible, both standing on tiptoes trying to support the tower, pressing against it with their little hands. That did stop the wobble on one side, only for it to start on the other.

"Hurry," the girl sighed. "I am not sure how much longer we can hold this in place."

The boy glanced over to the windowsill. The edges of the slates protruded slightly from the roughly plastered wall. He pressed one hand against the wall and then lifted his other shoulder high above his ear, as far as his body would let him.

His fingers touched the ledge, but only just.

But no matter how far he stretched, he was always an inch or so short of where he wanted to be. His heart started beating fast now, blood shooting into his head.

The tower below started to shake vigorously.

"Jump," I encouraged him. "Jump, you only have one go at this."

Then, almost as if in slow motion, one of the old rotten crates started to cave in under the weight of the boy. Time was running out. The construction was about to collapse.

Just one go. That's all it needs.

The stack of boxes tumbled to the ground with a loud crash, and the noise could be heard as far as the marketplace. The two siblings managed to press themselves into a doorway so as not to be hit by the falling boxes. Then, as they looked up, they saw the boy hanging on the slated ledge. Holding on with just one hand, his legs and feet dangling vigorously. They could hardly watch up to the events unfolding, but there was no need to worry. The boy, just like all the other children from the valley, was well used to this, dangling from trees and mountain ledges, and thus he swung his legs sideways and put his second hand onto the ledge to push himself up. As he did so with all his might, he quickly found a seat on the window ledge.

He grinned down at the boy and the girl, who in turn started clapping and stamping their feet in much delight. Just as he wanted to call down and thank them for their help, one of the merchants came running down the alley.

"And what do you think you are doing here? Ruining my lovely boxes."

Shaking both fists in the air, he shouted insults after the two fleeing children who were running away in search of a new hiding place.

The merchant turned around and started stacking his boxes into a neat pile.

The boy on the ledge observed the goings on from his position of relative safety. He felt a slight upset that he didn't have the chance to thank and say farewell to the children—especially since he had not met that many nice people on his travels, only the weaver woman, the clockmaker and the two siblings.

This is not great, he thought. *The town is full of people, but you stand more chance of meeting someone nice in an alpine hut than you do here.*

He thought back to the days when he used to drive the goats towards the luscious grasslands high up on the mountains. He would often spend the night in one of the alpine huts, especially when the weather was bad. All on his own with just a candle for light, whilst his father went out looking for a stray goat.

He had felt safer there than he felt now, and when he was there, he had never felt alone.

It wasn't until he had spent time in the town that he knew how terrible loneliness felt.

"I think you may meet them again," I remarked.

"You think so?"

"Perhaps."

"Then I will make it up to them and help them as best as I can," said the boy. And with this thought in mind, he climbed through the open window and landed on the half-landing of a spiral staircase.

The steps were made from white marble of the very expensive sort, the one embedded with tiny specks that sparkled like little crystals.

As his sore feet touched the cold stone, the boy closed his eyes in delight. He could feel the pain receding and was able to stand comfortably on his feet again. He felt how the tension eased from his knees and his ankles, and he sucked the cool air from inside the building deep into his lungs.

It was only now that he noticed how hot it had been outside. His shirt was sticking to his skin, but this came as no surprise, especially after that eventful morning. He had made his way through half the town, then the narrow escape from the policeman and next the successful negotiation of the wobbly tower. All this did not seem to matter at first but then, as he stood there for a minute or three, the cool air and his exhaustion made him shiver. A shiver ran between his shoulder blades all the way down his spine. The boy shook himself just like a dog that had come in from the wet.

Clack – Clack – Clack – Clack…

There! There was that noise again!

It came from the next floor, then wandered away not to be heard, at least for now. *Those shoes,* the boy thought, *they brought me luck. Without them I would still be standing around in that dark alley or walking around the building trying to gain entry, or even worse, getting caught by the gatekeeper.*

It was as if an invisible band was pulling him. He could not stop himself checking out the other floor, arriving only to find a long, almost endless corridor, wood panelled on either side. It seemed to run through the whole building. Portraits hung on both sides, portraits of old men painted in heavy oils, pictures that had been hanging there since the opening of the school. Some of them were so old that they had dulled, displaying a tear here and there, for after all they were just as impermanent as the faces they depicted. The boy did not notice them. He only focused on his long shadow reflecting on the highly polished parquet flooring. At the same time, he looked down at his feet, and suddenly he felt dirty and scruffy.

A cool breeze hit his sweaty shirt.

He rushed towards the middle of the corridor, where he had seen a classroom door slightly ajar. And with every step he took, he left behind a trail of sand, sweat and footprints.

"Sit up, listen up."

Amongst all the mumbling, clear words were audible, commanding the class. Very clear and direct words in fact. The boy was watching his shadow as it was almost twice as long as he was tall by now, and he did not want it appearing through the open door. Whatever went on behind this door, he would have to be careful if he ever wanted to find out.

"Put your hands together and keep your mouths shut."

Once again, he could hear the words echo through the corridor. The voice behind the door sounded serious and somewhat mean.

Best not to make a noise, the boy thought watching his shadow even more as not to be detected.

Just as the tip of his shadow reached the door, he quickly turned to the side and pressed himself against the panelled wall, causing his shadow to disappear and giving him chance to peek into the room. Now he could see where all the mumbling came from.

He stared at a row of benches placed along one wall, about a dozen of them. Filled with rows of children, well-clothed, almost looking like adults, wearing shirts and ties. Their heads were tilted towards their desks and their hands were clasped together.

They were reciting a verse.

On the single large desk in front of them pieces of chalk, a blackboard, and a sponge.

The teacher was standing in the middle of the room, addressing his class. His ruler swinging to the rhythm of the verse, almost as if he conducted a musical piece, eyes staring intently at a leather-bound book.

The mumbling stopped and the children looked expectantly at their teacher. The silence was almost deadly. A little boy pulled out his handkerchief and blew his nose.

"Quiet, listen up," thundered the teacher again and the little boy hastily returned his handkerchief to his pocket. Silence returned to the room. *They look like puppets*, thought the boy. *The way they are sitting there, motionless and stiff.*

"Lesson Fifteen, Verse One," the teacher thundered. "Proceed."

The ruler came crashing down on his desk, starting off the next round of mumbling.

This school is a strange place, thought the boy. The children were about his age but had nothing in common with the happy bunch of kids he knew from home. Life

79

for the kids at home was carefree and joyous, because the adults knew that it would turn serious soon enough. It was beneficial to have a joyous childhood, for the memory would be one of comfort once life takes a more serious turn.

The pupils are moving to the rhythm of the ruler, thought the boy, and had to briefly look away to distract himself from his perception. And when he looked again, it seemed to him that these children did not look like little children anymore, but like a row of little workers who moved and acted as expected.

They were all wearing the same clothes, and anything outside the power of the ruler seemed to be non-existent. The boy shook his head. *I am in the wrong place here,* he thought. *What now?*

"Wait," I said to him, and quickly called my old friend Fate.

"For what?"

"For Fate, my friend," I said. "For Fate."

Outside, the sun was already disappearing behind the high-rise buildings. She had done her work for today and was about to hand over to the moon.

Time for pupils and teachers alike to return home.

Clack – Clack – Clack – Clack …

There they were again. Those stiletto heels. Their sound was getting louder and louder. The boy, still pressing himself against the wooden panels by the open door, was unsure in which direction to escape.

The way across to the spiral staircase would lead back to the open window, but then what? It was impossible to get back into the alley from there. It would mean that he would have to jump, and for that it was far too high.

The other end of the corridor did not look promising either. And the turn offs to the left and right, well they could lead to anywhere. To another classroom, a stairwell, or even a dead end.

That leaves me no option but to try the jump, he thought, and tiptoed back towards the spiral staircase. Slowly at first, but then faster and faster, for the noise of the stiletto heels came closer and closer. He had only just set foot on the stairs when, as fate would have it, he bumped into a red skirt.

The force of the sudden obstacle threw him to the floor and onto his elbow. He winced in pain, and instinctively pressed his arm tight against his chest in an attempt to find some relief.

"Ouch," he groaned, "my arm."

And before he even realised that he had bumped into a human being, he heard a gentle voice.

"Goodness me. Where did *you* spring from?"

The boy rubbed his wet eyes and then pressed his arm against his body once more. It seemed to ease the pain. He noticed the bright red skirt and did not dare look up to see who it belonged to. He knew he had been caught out. He didn't belong here after all.

The figure in the red skirt looked down on him, as he was trying to hide his face.

A boy from the street, she thought.

There were plenty of them in this town, especially since the big factories had taken over and the adults did nothing but work.

But the figure did not try to ponder over the fate of those street kids, for she felt just like the others: To see those children was painful, and not looking meant not knowing, and therefore, the easiest option. But that was wrong, and she knew that too, and she was not proud of her actions.

I wonder how he got in here, she thought and bent down to stroke his back.

"Is it very painful?" she asked.

The boy twitched as he felt the strange hand which had little experience with what it did and he peeked through his fingers only to notice her blonde locks, then her eyes and how they searched the floor following his footprints towards the corridor. The shiny floor was covered in dirt and as she looked down on him, she knew where the dirt had come from.

What if the headmaster sees this, the figure thought, and started wondering how to best get rid of the boy. Getting rid because it would be the easiest option. But wasn't it too late for that?

The sounding school bell brought an end to all the thoughts and contemplations.

Hundreds of little hands suddenly stashed away pieces of chalk, blackboards and other learning materials, only to jump up from their seats and hastily make for the exit, almost as if they were being chased.

The eyes of the figure were still staring down the corridor. There was only one solution to the upcoming dilemma, and that was to run. So, she grabbed the boy by the scruff of his neck and started pulling him with her as fast as her stiletto heels would let her. Up the spiral staircase, past the opening doors, up to the next floor, where the next group of children had just begun leaving their classrooms, and where they could remain hidden in the crowd. The boy had trouble keeping up with her pace, the pace of a mad woman pulling on him as if he was today's prey. All he could see was the flashing colours; white, red, white, red, until he suddenly stumbled and rolled across a dark oak floor and came to a halt under one of the dormer windows.

As the figure pushed across it with her back, the door to the spiral staircase flung shut with a loud bang.

It seemed as if the figure wanted to keep danger at bay. Only now the boy finally noticed who he was dealing with. In front of him stood a young mistress, end twenties, dressed in a red skirt and a white blouse with shoulder-length blonde hair.

Her face was full of fear, her knees shaking. Her kind eyes indicated to the boy that he was safe and not at all a day's prey. On the contrary, he felt a sudden inner calm, a feeling he had forgotten about since the tycoon had visited his parents' house.

The noise on the lower floors started to fade, with only the teachers and the auxiliary staff remaining. One stood outside his classroom door, scratching his head with a miserable expression, wondering who had brought all the dirt into the school.

He called for the caretaker and told him to quickly restore the corridor to its usual sparkle.

It was exactly that call that echoed right up into the

attic and straight into the ears of the young miss, who suffered a terrible fright upon hearing it.

The boy realised that it must be associated with a bad memory from the past.

"The place where knowledge lives." The boy interrupted any unwanted thoughts and the silence that had followed them. "I have to find it."

His words came slow and thoughtfully, just like the words of a mother who soothes her child after a bad dream. And the voice he used was exactly the opposite to that of the miserable teacher.

The Miss stopped shaking and the signs of fear disappeared from her forehead.

"Is this where knowledge lives?" asked the boy.

But before he found the answer another creaking floorboard could be heard somewhere in the building, a slight summer breeze rattled the dormer window, then the building fell silent.

"What lives here?"

"Knowledge." The boy slowly spelled out every syllable, and with such an urgency that only a *yes* could be the answer.

Miss looked at the floor and then, slowly but surely, made her way to a large, winged chair and let herself fall into it with a big sigh.

"I only know of one person that calls this the place of knowledge," she said, and crossed one leg over the other. "It's been a while, but he used to come here often."

"The clockmaker?" asked the boy.

"You know him?"

"He sent me."

"To me?"

"Yes," he lied, and suddenly he noticed that the whole attic was full of books. Shelf after shelf, right to the very end of the vast room.

"He's read all the books no one else ever asked for," said the woman. "He wanted to build something and…"

"He *has* built it," the boy interrupted. "I've seen it and helped him whilst I was learning everything about the origin of time."

Miss looked at the boy.

He was so different compared to the other children in school. He was still raw, not yet formed, almost vulnerable. Like a proper child. He seemed to be different to the other street kids, even though he was just as scruffy. She could see that he didn't just live for the day. *He knows what he wants,* she thought, *and he is prepared to give it his all. He will take what they throw at him, just like I did.*

It had always been her ambition to become a teacher, even in a town where all official positions went to men, regardless of how conscientious the women were. She had tried everywhere and anywhere to get a position, even in the School of Music. And they had all sent her packing, despite her talent for languages, numbers, and arts.

"This is not a position befitting a woman," she was told, and at this school the headmaster had told her: "That's the way it is and that's the way it will stay." Instead he had offered her a position as a librarian, and that was how she'd ended up where she was now.

Better than nothing, she had thought, and she had

been waiting for a chance to become a teacher ever since. But that change had yet to come. All she would do was gather the ordered books together and deliver them to the teachers. And every evening, she would collect them again and return them to their respective places on the shelves, every single day without fail. She wouldn't even receive a thank you.

Thus, she lost herself in her little empire full of books as often as she would dare, sometimes until deep into the night. Page for page, losing herself in accounts of knowledge of the life that would remain unreachable outside these walls, often only with a candle by her side.

"I know all about time and all about health," said the boy. "But that will not be enough."

"Enough? For what?" asked the librarian.

"To save what I hold dear."

And with that, his gaze wandered over to the window and he began telling his story, about his family, the mean tycoon, how he had run away to find a solution, about the weaver woman and the clockmaker, and about his walk through the town in search for the place of all knowledge.

He chatted and chatted, just like a child who didn't care if someone was actually listening, a child adamant to take his fate into his own hands. There was no doubt in his words, and—the librarian thought—no doubt about where he took the faith from, especially since hers had left her a long time ago. She inspected him from top to bottom and noticed his sore, bleeding feet. *That must be terribly painful for him,* she thought.

She knew all about aching feet, her own trapped in

those stiletto heels all day long. How glad she was when she could exchange the heels for her slippers at night. She also noticed the streaks on his legs, where the running sweat had drawn little lines through the dirt.

"What if I *can't* help you?" she said, and immediately felt appalled at herself for seeking an excuse that fitted so well with turning a blind eye.

Appalled at herself that deep down inside, she had become one of those people she found despicable.

The boy seemed unimpressed, he continued to talk about how the clockmaker had told him there were three things he needed to master to perfection if he were to have even the slightest chance.

First, the ability to read. Second, the ability to write, and third, the ability to do maths. All other things that were to follow he would be able to teach himself, at the place where knowledge lived.

"And now that I have found this place," he said. "I am prepared to knuckle down and learn as much and as fast as I can."

He stood up, jammed his fists into his sides and looked the librarian straight in the eye, saying, "Come on, you. I'm ready for what there is to come."

The last rays of sunshine had already disappeared from the dormer windows and rung in the end of the day. The lanes and alleys were covered in darkness. The young miss was well aware of it and her heart was pounding.

What am I waiting for? she thought. *This is my chance to teach. The chance I have been waiting for. It's here but it is not permitted. It will go against all the rules of the school and against the teaching patriarchy. If I ever get discovered, they will throw me out. If I am lucky, that is.*

She began to shake once more, first her fingertips and then her whole body. Her cheeks reddened by the thought of fear, and I began to realise that she was torn between what was good and true, and the coldness which her heart had become accustomed to.

I took the opportunity to whisper into her ear.

"See where the path of fear has led you; imagine where you can go with me by your side…"

The boy had not budged an inch. It was just his shadow that had slowly moved over to the winged chair as the rays of the disappearing sun faded away. The librarian's gaze rested on the tail end of it, and she had become quite calm—so still in fact, that not even her chest dared to rise under the burden of her lungs as they breathed.

"Ready when you are," the boy repeated for the third time, now more adamant than ever.

At that very moment, the librarian got out of the chair and walked over to one of the shelves. She picked up an old leather-bound book with heavy iron mountings, dusted it off and flicked through it until she found a particular page. Her finger ran across the writing, then she closed the book and looked at the boy.

"I am…" the boy said, before she interrupted him gently.

"Me too," she replied, with a smile. "Me too."

CHAPTER 7

Knowledge

*Before you seek knowledge, ask yourself
about the purpose of your quest*

The hot summer was followed by a very cold winter. People always seemed to like the cold at first, for it brought a welcome relief after the hot summer days. But as the days start to get shorter and shorter and the icicles hanging from the windowsills longer and longer, they condemn the cold just as quickly as the searing heat. Much to the dismay of the weather gods who—most upset about the way mankind treats nature—decided to prolong the cold season well into the middle of spring. It was then followed by a dry summer and a wet autumn, making the already sparse crops on the fields rot away.

During those times, whenever humans raised their heads up to the sky to observe the weather, all they could see were dark clouds and swarms and swarms of birds migrating south. And when the clouds finally broke again and the last of the birds had gone, the people knew very well what the coming winter would bring.

"I am going to put them to bed," said the mother.

"Is it paining them much?" asked the father.

"Yes," she replied.

"It be will easier once they are asleep; they will not feel it so much then."

But they will dream of it, thought the mother, trying to smile at the father, who in turn was trying his utmost to keep hunger away from his loved ones.

"Let us go easy with what we have got," he said. "There will be better times soon."

The mother nodded and turned around, tears in her eyes.

The father stretched his hand out to her and said, "Come." His gesture was that of a man who had been totally overwhelmed by the theatre of life, and who was indeed very scared of the next act that was there to come.

He let his arm fall to the side when he did not get a reaction.

"I just cannot cope with this," said the mother quietly. "What kind of mother am I if all I can offer my children are tears?"

The father's eyes welled up, but he had learned to control this emotion. He walked over to the wooden cupboard, opened the door and picked up the already dry loaf of bread. He pulled his penknife out of his trouser pocket, undid the safety catch and held the knife in his right hand. The bread tightly pressed to his chest, he cut three wafer-thin slices and laid them onto a white cloth.

"Here," he said to his wife. "Take my part of tonight's dinner."

"But…" she hesitated.

"Never mind. Give it to the children."

The mother stroked her husband's free hand and kissed him on his already gaunt cheeks before she took the little offering.

In the children's bedroom, the little brother was restless in his cot. He was tired, very tired in fact, but there was something missing to send him to the land of nod. His two sisters stood beside his cot, looking down at the mini-human in disbelief, not quite comprehending how a little mite like him could squeal that much and with such persistence.

They were thinking about the reasons for why he was crying. Was he having teething problems, or did his nappy need changing?

Or did he just want another cuddle? *If only we knew what is bothering him so much,* thought the two sisters, pressing their hands against their ears.

"Our little one is hungry," their mother explained. She had quietly entered the bedroom and walked towards the cot. A few soft gestures sent the girls back to their beds before she opened the white linen cloth and broke the bread into small pieces.

She started putting the little pieces into the boy's mouth, and with his hunger satisfied, he stopped squealing. Next it was the girls' turn, and the mother stroked their heads until they finally fell asleep, snuggled up between the mattress and the duvets like two little angels.

She walked over to the window where another bed was situated. This bed had been empty for quite some time now and would remain empty this night too. The mother picked up the pillow to shake it and fluff it, then she smoothed the sheets with the back of her hand. She did this every day, twice a day in fact, once in the morning and once in the evening.

This bed had belonged to her eldest son before he had left home. A silent witness would have dismissed this ritual as unnecessary, but the mother's motivation lay deeper. As she smoothed the sheets down, she looked out of the window and up into the sky. She thought about her boy with whom she had bonded when he was still kicking about in her tummy. She had brought him up and never wasted a thought about how life would be if he ever were to leave home. But leave he did.

Where was he?

I am standing here unable to help him, she thought, *but I'll make his bed every day, so he will feel at home when he comes back. Back to where his roots are and to all that he holds dear.*

She looked up to the moon which had just appeared behind a black cumulus cloud. Its light dipped the valley into a deep blue and grey.

All was quiet across the fields and in the houses. Only the wind could be heard how it was blowing the golden October leaves across the ground, towards the next obstacle where they accumulated and stayed until the next snowfall pressed them to the ground.

"Are you looking at the moon too, my boy?" the mother whispered into the sky.

How beautiful the moon is, she thought, *more so than the sun, which you could never observe fully because it would burn your eyes. The moon is preferable to me,* she thought, *especially with all its sobriety and peacefulness.*

"He'll look after you, my dear child," she whispered quietly. "Wherever you may be."

She placed her fingertips to her lips, kissed them, and then blew the kiss high up to the moon where it circled around the dark side, the side no one had ever seen before. Then it returned to Mother Earth, breaking through the clouds and heading straight for a source of light on the otherwise dark streets.

The light got bigger and bigger. The contours of the buildings illuminated, some big and magnificent made from steel and glass, but the kiss would not be impressed by such splendour. It travelled straight to the dormer window and settled next to an old oil lamp where a boy sat reading a book. With a blanket wrapped around his shoulders, he didn't even waste a thought on trying to find any sleep.

His eyes were firmly glued to the book, his finger gliding along the written lines, his lips moving to the rhythm of the written word, but silently.

The kiss did not hesitate. It carried on to find its destiny, past the lamp, to the end of its journey. The boy had just turned a page and moved on to a new chapter. He took a deep breath, read the first syllable and suddenly felt a slight tickle on his forehead.

"Mother?" he said. "Surely, it cannot be possible for you to be here?"

He listened out into the long vast room, and... silence. Nothing.

It's been more than a year, he thought, and stood up to look at the moon.

If you could see me now, here in my little empire, you wouldn't believe your eyes. And I would have so much to tell you about all the fantastic things I have learned and experienced, and all the books, my new friends, who surprise me every single day.

"You wouldn't believe," he added quietly.

I rest during the day, so as not to make any noise. I do not want to endanger the young Miss, my teacher, who is looking after me so well and selflessly, just the way you did when I was still at home. I can move freely at night, almost like a bird, and I dance with the letters and numbers and absorb all knowledge until the sun rises once more above the roof tops of the town. That is when I crawl back into my hiding place right at the very back of the room, behind the shelf with the old books written by the old masters, the ones that nobody looks at anymore. Apart from my teacher of course, whose daytime job is that of a librarian, but she is actually a teacher at heart.

She teaches the way the old folk did when they were still young and there was no one to give lessons, like in the good old times before schools and factories and all those things that dictate life these days. Before you seek knowledge, my teacher quoted an old master: "ask yourself about the purpose of your quest, for the unnecessary things rob us of our time."

And we all need to know the value of our time.

I have kept the clockmaker's note, and now that I have learned to read, I read it every day.

I have also learned to write, although my handwriting is not very neat.

But this week, I am able to write faster and better than I could last week, and because I'm not doing anything else but this, I am getting better and better with every hour I do not sleep.

"Have you gone to sleep, mother?" the boy asked. His chin resting on his fist, he gazed up to the moon. "I am sure your days are just as long as my nights, which I do not want to end. There is still so much to learn."

Another cloud had slowly started pushing in front of the moon, and darkness won over light.

With the disappearing moon, the tickle on the little boy's forehead stopped and a feverish restlessness took over.

I need to know what the tycoon knows, he thought, *otherwise I will not be able to stop him, and he will always get what he wants.*

The boy did not even have to try to remind himself of what the tycoon looked like. That was a face he would never forget.

"Enough dawdling," he reminded himself loudly, feeling strange at the same time. "I must not ponder about matters that do not bring me forward."

So, he tried to forget the moon, the tycoon, his mother and the kiss, but the latter was painful to dismiss, thus he felt a little pain in his chest. But he cut that off before it got into his mind. After the incident at the well on that fateful day, where our journey had nearly come to an end, he had gotten quite good at cutting off any emotions.

I must only think about the things that make me progress, thought the boy.

Everything else is pointless. If I can continue night by night, without any rest and any further ado, then maybe one day, something big will happen and I will not be able to explain why. I often fall asleep with a book in my arms, and in my dreams I clearly see the old masters standing in front of me with their rules and their teachings, with their maps of roads and rivers drawn onto old papyrus paper. I see their figures and how they are stacked under symbols, for then to be broken down until just a hundredth or even a thousandth of them remains.

I see the spoken word, how it clearly draws its lines, black on white and how it is awoken to sound by merely the movement of the mouth. Then late in the afternoon when my teacher wakes me, I often feel as if I already know all of this.

I could just continue tomorrow, he thought, as he turned away from the window. *It doesn't matter, and I have already achieved so much. Today, yesterday and the days before.*

"No!" He said, directing his words at the moon. "Every time you postpone something, you cheat on your time and your dreams will remain empty. That's if you are lucky. If you are unlucky, the dreams will fill with doubts and fear and the worried looks of father and mother."

That I don't want, thought the boy, and turned the wheel of his oil lamp far to the right, until the dark greenish light turned bright and yellow so it wouldn't hurt his eyes as much. His finger continued to slide over the words of the remaining chapter, doubly quick compared to what it would normally have done. Once finished, he closed the book, picked up his pencil and made a few notes on a piece of paper.

Then he picked up the sheets the teacher had prepared for him and brought with her to the library every Sunday. The work for the week was on those sheets. There were lists of books to read, the writing of essays, the solving of mathematical puzzles and a thousand other things that would make him progress, just as a tree would grow when you quench its thirst.

He started with a row of figures that had been causing him difficulties the day before. The multiplication sum seemed alright, so it must be the division that he had worked out previously. The result was doubtful, so he started again. Figure by figure, comma by comma, and when he finally spotted his mistake, it made him chuckle. The other maths exercises were constructed in a similar fashion and took little time to solve. Done and dusted.

He proceeded with the poetry exercise, quite entangled poetry to be totally honest with you. The first spoke of the blossoming and wilting in nature, the second of the constant fight between dark and light. The third spoke of ebb and flow.

The fourth remained a riddle, for it asked about mother and father, the origin of larger life, dictating contrasts that in the end turned out to be deeply entangled. The boy started chewing the end of his pencil and using his tongue, pushing it from one side of his mouth to the other, a habit he assumed when he was intently thinking about something.

He couldn't quite point his finger to when this had started, and to be honest with you, he didn't much care about it either. The only thing he knew was that this fad seemed to sharpen his senses, and the faster the pointed end moved to and fro, the quicker the little scraps of thought in his head would piece together until they gave him the answer he was looking for. But not always immediately. Sometimes, the picture was a little blurred at first, like a watercolour, and it took a while for the lines to become clearer. Sometimes, the lines appeared and then disappeared again, which angered the little boy. He would pull the pencil out of his mouth and stick it behind his ear and let the problem rest to address it the next day.

I have trust in such moments, thought the boy, *trust that time will let me solve what I couldn't solve the day before.*

The tip of the pen stopped right at the end of his nose.

This riddle is not one to be solved over two days, he thought.

I could see what was about to happen.

He did not only see the lines of two circles, one large, one small, but rather, he also saw the larger circle starting to shine bright yellow and the other turning grey with little graphite-coloured dots.

"Yes, of course," whispered the child to himself, writing the solution in the intended space on the exercise sheet and continuing to the next task in question. "Well, what have we here?"

The boy felt this strange rhythm inside, almost like

the beat of a tin drum, but it did not irritate him, instead it seemed to motivate him. And whilst the stars stood high in the sky, his inquisitive nature raced from one question to another.

The boy had only just finished a fable with the title 'The Little Oak' and was already holding the next in his hand. "This is my night," he said to himself, and once again felt a tad strange.

Is it strange, he thought, *if the mind breaks the rules and we let it?* No, it is not."

At least that was what his teacher once said: "Strange would be to follow the rules all the time. You could even call it appalling, albeit it's never the fault of the pupils that the grown-ups act like that, only because they were never allowed to be children themselves. But it also does not give them the right to leave their children under the influence of all the rules until their naivety has been completely destroyed. They take away more than they give, but you, you have been lucky."

"Lucky?" the boy had asked and raised an eyebrow.

"Yes, lucky," she had answered. "Because your path has not been drawn for you. You are lucky enough to be able to make the world your own."

That was all the boy needed to know.

During the first weeks of him living in the attic, he had watched the other schoolboys from the dormer window, looked on as they spilled into the marketplace at the end of each day.

"Do you envy them?" I had asked him.

All that they are and have. Their clothes and shoes,

the leather satchels with the golden crest. All the expressions of belonging to a better class of people. His expression indicated that he did.

What did he have to offer?

His roughly sewn pair of trousers made from leather. A shirt already patched far too many times. The naked soles of his feet?

But as soon as he understood the contents of the books his teacher had to arrange for these children's classes, his envy faded. They were all taught the same things, plenty of rules and regulations for how to be and how not to be. Endless verses that started with, "I must" or "I must not." There was another book available in the library, with the title, "I should" but that did not seem to be very popular with the teachers and was seldom requested.

I am lucky, the boy thought, looking along the rows of bookshelves and observing how they slowly disappeared into a section of *I want* and *What I desire, the things that make me progress.* Far more preferable than a satchel with a golden crest.

Again he looked out the window and noticed the beginnings of dawn appearing on the horizon.

Hurriedly, he put pen to paper, and by the time the first rays of sunlight broke through the dormer glass, his work was done. The rhythm of the tin drum had fallen silent and given way to the dreams that sometimes fell upon the boy without warning and stayed with him for much longer than they normally would.

He did not hear his teacher opening the door, finding her ward fast asleep in the winged chair. She quickly glanced down the spiral staircase, shut the door behind her, and removed her stilettos. Next she collected all the books and exercise sheets strewn all around him, witness to a busy night. The boy still held his pencil in his hand, the lead worn and rounded like one of his fingertips.

He has not budged an inch, thought the teacher. *He is sleeping where he dropped, and it will still be a while before he will rise from his sleep.*

She walked over to her desk and began to examine his homework, starting with the reading list.

She was astonished that he had already completed the list and she set about returning the books to their rightful places on the shelves.

She then went through the rows of maths exercises she had given him and ticked those off as completed too. The same with the essays, and subjects relating to questions of nature, foreign countries and history. The boy stirred, only to fall back into a deep sleep again.

The teacher continued her work, concentrating on the boy's writings. Every mistake she would find today was one the boy would not make tomorrow. For if you eliminate the mistakes, you will progress quicker in this game called life that we must not lose. By the time the boy finally opened his eyes, the autumn sun had almost gone.

The teacher had just finished her work and the boy was pleased to see the familiar face.

"You have done it child. It is achieved," she said.

The boy, still not quite awake, rubbed the sleep out of his eyes and sat upright in the winged chair. He pulled his feet up and wrapped both his arms around his legs, looking searchingly across the oak floor, where his pencil lay on his blanket.

"My exercise sheets. I wanted to sort them into the correct order," he mumbled.

"I've already done that," the teacher replied. She crossed one leg over the other and pressed her lips together, so they formed a small line.

The boy was irritated by her behaviour.

Have I done something wrong? he thought. *If I have, I will make up for it tonight. All I need is more oil for my lamp and to sharpen my pencil. I've had a good rest and the new night hasn't even started. I can study longer than I did last night.*

"What day is it today?" the teacher asked.

He ignored the question and was still staring at her tight lips, fighting the upcoming negative thoughts. *I have been too quick,* he thought. The night has been magical, but maybe also deceiving. Have I lost track with all those figures and words?

Or maybe not?

My dreams were so clear that I thought I had been awake at night. My limbs insisted on the opposite, and my mind seemed confused and full of nonsense.

"Wednesday, dear boy," said the teacher. "It is Wednesday."

Her fingertips rolled over his exercise papers all neatly piled up on the desk next to her. A collection of papers spanning a hand's width.

"Wednesday?" the boy asked, confused.

"Yes, Wednesday," the teacher repeated. "Your work

for seven days, complete in four."

And as she said it, her mouth suddenly relaxed and she walked over to the boy.

"Well, you know," she said, and found it difficult to find the right words, especially in a place where criticism and reprimands were more common than anything else.

"Your work is exemplary, truly exemplary. I have long been waiting for the day when *my* work would make a difference. But no one would let me. Well, not until you appeared."

The teacher pulled the boy off the chair and gave him a big hug. Warmth radiated from her heart and the boy could feel it beating against his chest.

He felt elated.

She tried to preserve the moment by closing her eyes. *I would rather not let go,* she thought, *but his time here is coming to an end. He knows what he needs to know, and he has learned how and where to obtain more knowledge. I must not put my happiness above his.*

"I am very, very proud of you," she whispered.

The boy looked at her peaceful face and pressed himself deeper into her soft chest. He felt one of her locks stroking his cheeks and took a deep breath to suck in the sweet air. He closed his eyes and listened to the heartbeat, feeling much happiness.

"Thank you," he said. "Thank you for everything." And then, after a long pause which seemed like eternity, he opened his eyes and froze.

"What on earth is going on?" a male voice suddenly rumbled from behind. "And where did this scruff bag come from?"

The teacher instantly sensed that the happiest day of her life had come to a sudden end as the headmaster's voice started thundering down at her. He had suddenly appeared in the doorway, clutching a pile of books, that had crashed to the floor as he set eyes on the boy. An intruder to his hallowed halls, that was how he saw it.

He clenched his fists and gritted his teeth, like a horse biting into an apple. His eyes and his mouth spat poison, words that cannot be repeated here, words of the sort that can only come from a cold heart.

"Madam," he croaked, turning all his anger against the librarian, "Throw that thing out before I throw you out."

The teacher, who stopped being a teacher at this very moment in time, withstood the hatred and shielded the boy.

This in turn added fire to the already blazing flames. By now, the headmaster had gotten himself into such a rage that his head had turned bright red and large pearls of sweat appeared on his forehead.

"Madam," he scorned, "surely you are not...or are you?"

A shudder run down the librarian's back.

The little boy, still in a state of shock and unable to move or speak, witnessed the headmaster's fist rising into the air.

"I dare you, you pretence of a man," said the librarian with a loud voice—meaning that she saw him as a nobody without his gown and that silly mortarboard on top of his head.

"A skeleton is what you are. A ghost, nothing more. A ghost that torments little children and finds pleasure in it."

"You silly cow," the headmaster screamed, and set his spindly legs in motion to leap at the disobeying woman.

The boy, watching closely, tore himself away from her and ran headfirst towards the headmaster.

A split second later, he had rammed into the hips of the man, then somersaulted sideways only to land on the floor of the staircase. The headmaster could just about follow the shadow disappearing through the doorframe, but not before an attempt at blocking the door with his foot. His foot, however, was no match for the old oak doorframe and it took only seconds before it got the better of the very same. The three heard his bones splinter into little pieces.

The headmaster had incapacitated himself.

"Run, boy, run," the librarian shouted after him, whilst the headmaster was still wondering why his right leg wouldn't support him anymore.

The boy hesitated. "I don't want to leave you here like this," he begged.

"You will have to, child. You will have to!"

There was no going back.

No warm chest, no shielding arms, and once the boy had come to terms with the new situation, he raced down the white marble staircase accompanied by the loud cries of the headmaster, who was in such pain that he nearly fainted.

The boy managed to leave a floor behind him, racing downstairs that quickly that the oiled banister rails almost burned streaks into his hands. Just before he managed to descend to another flight, he could see the caretaker heading his way.

Alarmed by the noise and all the screaming, the man felt compelled to come to the aid of those who summoned help.

Ah, there he is, the scruff bag, barefoot as well! Must be a thief, the caretaker thought, swinging his broom in direction of the child.

The boy took the obstacle as a challenge and quickly jumped down the next three steps and let himself drop to the floor, only to slide underneath the broom and straight through the wide-open legs of the caretaker—just as a penguin slides down an icy slope. He stopped just short of a bucket of water.

The boy knew that all the corridors led to a dead end. The only way out was via the marble staircase, but that led past the gatekeeper who watched over the exit day and night. The boy did not waste a thought over how to get past him; he would tackle that when he came to it.

He was watching the caretaker, how he headed towards him, his broom jammed under his arm with the pointed end first and aiming straight for the boy's head like a knight carrying a lance—but without his horse. His huffing and puffing destroyed every chance of a fair duel. First, he trotted and then eventually sprinted towards the boy, who suddenly spotted his opportunity.

Grabbing the bucket, he released a wave of water

that would stop the pseudo-knight dead in his tracks. Then he tiptoed through the puddle, carefully but with determination.

The caretaker was not quite as lucky. He approached the puddle with such a speed that he started to slip on first contact. One leg flew up in the air, arms heavily rowing against gravity. He landed on his bottom with one almighty splash, the broom sliding down the hallway seconds later.

I've done it, thought the boy, grabbing hold of the banister and descending the marble staircase to the safety of the exit. Lungs pumping, he now set eyes on the gatekeeper storming from his gatehouse, arms wide open, trying to catch hold of the boy.

"Run, run," the librarian shouted over to him from afar, and the boy picked up pace.

He made it through the gate into the marketplace, and just as he intended to slow down, he noticed that he was being followed and could hear the steps coming closer and closer.

I wonder how big the gap is between him and me? the boy thought. *Better not look back, I might loose all the advantage. Run, just run. If my legs can carry me from home to town, they'll help me escape.*

"You fool," disagreed his legs. "You did not look after us during your book exile."

And indeed, the boy could feel how his legs were getting weaker with every step.

The merchant houses may have come closer, but the steps behind him were gaining too.

In addition to the steps, he could also hear a beastly

wheeze. The boy thought he could feel someone breathing down his neck and he started to scream.

The sound travelled over the empty marketplace into the dark alleys and echoed back.

I need to keep going, he thought. *Do not give up. No far now.* He was looking for the dark emptiness signalling the entrance to one of the alleys, leading to God know where. *Just need to get away from this bloodhound chasing me,* he thought.

The boy put all his eggs into one basket, delving into the dark without knowing what lay behind it.

The hunted had escaped the hunter.

The boy brushed along the rough walls of a dark alley which first veered off to the left, then to the right, and opened up into a small courtyard with three small alley leading off. The boy turned off and travelled against his previous direction to ensure that he would finally shake of his pursuer.

Mustn't make a sound, he thought, and began to slow down. That took the strain off his lungs, and he was eventually able to listen out for any noises.

He could hear footsteps from across the road. They stopped for a moment, appearing to turn around and fade away into the dark. The alley fell silent, and the boy suddenly realised how tired he was.

He let himself drop to the floor, pleased to finally be alone. *Finally,* he thought. *Peace and quiet.*

He was not privy, however, to the librarian stepping into the marketplace, her face bright red, but not wasting any tears; she was too proud to show any weakness to the hoodlums chasing her away.

Her belongings trailed behind her as she walked out of the gate with her head held high, and the caretaker was throwing the rest after her.

A framed picture of a flower, a beautifully decorated cup, the oil lamp, all landing on the cobble stones, lying there in tatters just like her future.

But she didn't care, because she had learned not to look away anymore, and from now on, she would be driven by the good—and only the good.

"You scoundrels," she shouted back, and kicked her feet, which in turn caused the caretaker to retreat back into the building. And long before the gatekeeper had returned from his nightly prowl, she had gone home, thinking about the boy who was once again all on his own.

CHAPTER 8

Strength

We all have it in us, it just needs to be unleashed

Further down, in the web of lanes and alleys, the boy had managed to get a little rest. His legs were still not as strong as they used to be, leaving him with a feeling of exhaustion, just as the whole town seemed to exhaust him. It seemed to be wearing him out.

The sun had already disappeared into the horizon, the town had calmed down and the hustle and bustle had turned into the odd person stumbling home from the pub and the occasional coach or carriage rumbling across the cobble stones with the dim street lanterns lighting the way. But that was nothing unusual and the boy did not take much notice.

I can't stay here, he thought. *Sooner or later, I will run straight into the arms of a night watchman, or even a drunk*

And then what?

And as he was pondering over his next move, he noticed the cold creeping up on him. He got off the floor and wrapped his arms around his waist in an attempt to keep himself warm.

He pulled his shoulders up as far towards his ears as possible, but his head and his legs remained unprotected and the cold hit him with all its might.

This comfort I enjoyed throughout the last year has made me soft, he thought. Soft against the force of nature. Nature does not care if a man is dressed up warm or a boy does not possess a pair of shoes.

I could really do with a coat now, he thought, *and a pair of shoes.* But then there are lots of things I could do with for the upcoming winter. Perhaps there is still time before the arrival of father frost, for by the time the frost arrives I will hopefully have found myself a warm fire and not having to spend the nights underneath the open sky.

Hopefully, it's not going to start raining, he thought, although looking at the clouds that had enshrouded the moon and sensing the smell of damp in the air, it was most certainly going to. *Can it not rain until tomorrow or the day after? By then I will have found myself another roof over my head.*

Yes, the boy thought. *Tomorrow or the day after will suffice. For nature and for me.*

He had only just finished this thought when a raindrop hit this left ear. And then another, running down his neck and slowly soaking into his greatly patched shirt.

"Uh-oh," he cursed. "Why…?"

"Why you?" I interrupted.

"Yes, why me?"

"Because bad things always come in threes," answered.

"First, they wanted to smack you around the head then they threw you out of the house and hunted you through the streets, and now it is starting to rain. And everything you have will be drenched in no time. You will be soaked right to the skin and your knees will start shaking and your lips will turn blue, because you will feel cold. Very cold indeed."

He looked at me in disbelief, as if I had held a mirror up to him. "Do you want to know what will happen next? I asked.

He didn't.

"You will become ill. Without a roof over your head without your mother, all on your own in this strange town You will constantly be busy protecting yourself, and what do you think will eventually give way?"

There was no need for me to speak any further. I said everything I could. What else would have fired up his self pity on this rainy autumn night?

Nothing.

So, I said, "Self-pity does not keep you warm, nor does it provide you with food and neither will it help you save what is dear to you. It only numbs. It numbs the spirit and the body, until it is too late."

"Too late?" mumbled the boy.

"Only if you don't get a move on," I answered.

A little trickle of water ran down the boy's cheeks. I

had dripped from his hair.

He finally noticed that he was already soaked through to the skin with his teeth chattering from the cold. He stood up, stuffed his hands deep into his pockets and made his way down the alley until he got to a lane.

He followed the lane until he reached a street junction and then he turned right.

Seeking shelter from the rain under the trees, he looked around for lit windows, for something inviting, a door or window he could knock on.

He heard music coming from one of the villas, even fragments of conversations here and there. He saw the glowing ends of lit cigars. Two figures were leaning against a door frame, laughing and joking. Opposite them, behind a huge glass window, a dozen or more people could be seen, sitting around a big dining table richly filled with a formidable turkey and other fine foods. The clothes of the attendees were noble and magnificent. A maid served tray after tray laden with delicacies, tracked by the hungry eyes of the boy. But the guests ignored the feast. All their attention was focused on the sparkling necklaces, pearls and rings and other tinsel that decorated their décolletés, hands and ears.

"I must get one of those," he heard a lady say, pointing towards the large ruby on the finger of her adversary.

"A unique piece," the other answered.

"Fortunately!"

The fake smile on her lips and her raised eyebrows spoke of her satisfaction at how she had put the other firmly in her place.

The lady in question understood the signs. Sh
smiled politely and looked accusingly at her husband. H
in turn did not understand his wife's sudden mood swin
and tried to cheer her up.

"Look darling," he said. "Let's have some turkey. I
looks delicious."

"And why would I want some of that stupid bird?
she snapped at him. "I want glamour, not this commo
stuff."

The husband was just about to object, even thoug
he knew that any attempt would be pointless, when th
host of the party raised his glass for a toast.

A short speech later, the anger had passed and th
party returned to gossip and scandal once more.

The boy watched the goings-on from a shadow of
tree.

All this food, he thought. *If only…*

But the rain, by now falling heavily from abov
reminded him that he had to keep moving. He left th
villas behind and arrived in an area of the town where th
labourers lived.

There wasn't much to see here, one house like th
next, and almost all appearing like upside-down shoeboxe
small and dreary. The streets were dull and grey; there wa
not much here at all, and the boy made his way throug
the streets quite quickly. At first, he was still able to war
off the rain, walking underneath the overhangs of some o
the roofs, but then the wind changed direction and cam
from the side, quickly soaking into the last remainin
dry patches of his shirt and trousers. It rained that har

now that he had to keep wiping the raindrops out of his eyes. The rain had turned into a torrential downpour that hammered its way down relentlessly.

Water, the boy thought, *first from above, then from the side. And now it won't be long before it will also rise from the ground.*

"If this carries on, he said aloud, but to himself, the town will drown and so will I."

It was impossible to hear his voice, that's how hard the rain was coming down.

Shelter, he thought. *I must find some shelter. Somewhere dry and warm and light. And until I've found such a place, I will need to keep moving, otherwise it will not only be my feet that will be numb, but my hands and my head too. Must keep feeling my nose. If I can't feel myself pinching my nose anymore, then God help me.*

And thus, he turned the next corner with the hope of finding something suitable to ease his misery.

He let his eyes wander along the road and was convinced he had walked around the town in a complete circle.

Hopefully, I'll find something once I get to the end of the road, he thought. *Just a little bit further.*

He carried on walking. But at the end of the road, the next was exactly like the first and the boy began to curse the town. The frontages of the little shoeboxes were starting to look like prison walls. Grey, high and impassable. Especially for all those who were not in possession of the right key.

Well, best carry on, he thought, rubbing his cold, wet

hands together. "Keep going, legs." He tried to encourage himself. "Not far now. I can feel it. We're nearly there."

The boy ran as fast as he could, but even the most vigorous movement could not keep him warm anymore. His teeth chattering, his lips blue, the hand of the clock had already moved to midnight and the boy knew that the temperature would drop even further.

Usually, in the early hours of the morning, just before the sun is due to rise, that's the lowest point, thought the boy. *I must find myself a hole to crawl into before then, otherwise I might not make it. Not in this storm, not in this weather.*

He wiped the raindrops from his lashes for what must have been the hundredth time.

Nearly at the end of the road… just a little bit further. Just a teeny bit.

He arrived at another crossroads and stopped. It all looked the same. Grey houses to the left, grey houses to the right. Row after row. No trees, no bushes, no foliage. Only a dripping wet and by now very desperate boy, whose time was slowly running out.

Necessity is the mother of invention.

"Knock on the doors," I said. "All of them, just like the last time you were in the suburbs."

"But what if it goes wrong?" the boy stuttered knowing he didn't have much choice.

"Go on, before the flood washes you away."

He stopped at the next door and rapped the knocker as hard as he could.

Tock – Tock – Tock

The iron ring hammered against the door, but

nothing. He walked a few steps and tried the next door, again and again until he had tried more than half of the houses in the road to no avail. He could feel his nose getting numb.

Tock – Tock – Tock

"Open up, someone. Please."

But all the shouting and begging he could muster didn't produce the wanted result. Not a soul opened their door for him, and so he continued walking until he reached a fast-flowing river. A small bridge, hung from steel ropes, a crossing—albeit a dangerous one. The boy observed the bridge swinging in the storm.

This must be the edge of this district, he thought. *A border between one district and the next. Without high walls and closed doors.*

Maybe there is a forest on the other side of the river, somewhere where I can crawl under a pile of leaves, just like the hedgehogs do. Somewhere to stay until this night is over. Somewhere to spend the night until I can try my luck again tomorrow.

"You fool," he said to himself. "You've been wrong all evening. You didn't get anywhere and have been searching the whole night, running from one road to another. Luck has left you. It doesn't matter anymore what you do. What if there is no forest on the other side of the river? What if there are the highest mountains or the deepest seas on that side, or something else a boy like me can't master?"

His lips chattered so much now that he was unable to utter another word.

He lifted his wet shirt by the neckline and blew warm

air under it, and then he looked up at the black clouds tha
were pushing each other along, looking at how they kep
interlocking and relieving themselves of more and mor
rain. They had already filled the river to the brim, makin,
the water gush along the riverbed at such a speed that n
one would be able to control it.

If I fall in, the boy thought, *then it's goodnight, m
friend.* A sudden warmth flowed through his body, but th
boy took fright at the mere thought of even thinking abou
the end.

Summoning all the strength he had left, he jumpe
onto the bridge, his hands firmly grabbing hold of the stee
wire. The wire felt cold, the bridge was slippery under foo
and the sudden warmth had disappeared just as quickly a
it had arrived.

"Look," I said to him, almost shouting in his ear, "u_l
there, behind the clouds…"

A red glow had appeared in the darkness, a cloak o
light, pulsing in tune with the hammering rain.

The boy had endured much more of the cold tha
he had thought. His hands, feet and nose were numb an
now his mind seemed to be playing tricks on him too. I
seemed as if fog had clouded his thoughts.

My legs are still going, he thought. *It's almost a miracle
but they are still working. They will carry me towards the re
glow. It's not far. Just a little bit further. Just a teeny bit more*

Nobody knew when the green flatlands had firs
been populated. A long time ago, that was for sure, bu
when exactly, no one seem to remember.

Old fables spoke of nomads who had sought shelte

and lush meadows for their herds. There were also tales of a large ford on the river, apparently once used by the herdsmen until one day, when someone decided to settle at that very spot.

The residents of the town couldn't care less.

They did not start counting time until the first furnace was built. In comparison to the one that now dominated the town, it must have been fairly small, but it sowed the seed for the rest that would later occupy the north of the town. It alone had been the origin of the wealth that followed. The ore molten in this furnace had forged the first tools.

And these tools in turn had helped to work the fields which had caused a flow of people to move to the by then prosperous flats.

The settlement had grown into a rich town, its unstoppable rise beating to the rhythm of the machines, wheels and furnaces. Before long, thick black clouds and fog hung above this industrious part and the rich and wealthy moved to the south, into their palaces made from glass and steel. And not only that, but they also built villas and houses, schools and pubs and many other places. They even built a cathedral, a sign of reverence to their god. A duplicitous act, as some of the wealthy knew to report behind closed doors, for their eyes had not been watching God for quite some time. All their hopes and desires were set onto the thousand-degree hot fires instead. Fires that must never go out.

"As long as the north is glowing red," they were heard saying, "our larders will always be full."

And nothing else mattered for the foreseeable future

The boy had reached the middle of the bridge clinging onto the steel wire, well aware that it would b the end of him if he slipped and let go. Twenty feet below him was the gushing river, tossing and swirling, the bridg swinging from side to side in the storm like a raging bul tied by its nose. Care had to be taken with every step. Th ground was slippery and wet, the wind had become hi enemy, trying to push him away from the safety of th wire.

That glow must come from a fire, the boy thought. *man-made fire. Which other flame would be able to surviv in such a storm?*

"Warmth," he mumbled and took another step in th direction of that inviting glow. And whilst he moved hi weight from one foot to the other, it nearly knocked him over

I must work with the gusts, he thought, *not agains them. If only I could make two or even three steps at a time but then again, that will tear the wire out of my hands. So, it better to go gingerly and make the storm my friend. Yes, that how it shall be. Work with the odds rather than against them*

And just as he had finished his trail of thought, h passed the middle of the structure, and the bridge wa swinging less.

"Warmth," the boy mumbled to himself. He felt how the gusts had stopped, and seizing the moment, he took big leap forward. He waited for the next gust to pass an leapt forward again, and then a third time.

He heard something crash into the river below A water wheel had seemingly broken loose and wa crashing from side to side, driven by the countless swirls and undercurrents. Minutes later, parts of a former mill became visible, bobbing up and down and disappearing into the darkness.

The boy finally made it off the bridge and onto the cobbled towpath. He took a deep breath.

I'm back on solid ground, he thought, *even if my knees are about to give way.* He looked up and the glow appeared to be coming closer.

That, and that alone is enough for me to keep going, he thought.

He carried on, along a wall seemingly belonging to a factory. Next he climbed up a large coal mountain, never losing sight of his goal. Then he found himself sliding down the other side, where he faced a fence stopping him from getting further. At least three times as tall as himself, it was impossible to scale. He walked alongside it, looking for a loose plank or a gap he could fit through. Success. The rain did not let off as the boy bent the loose plank sidewards and crawled through the gap. It appeared the storm was going to continue throughout the night, and even though the howling wind was hindered by the vast number of buildings, the boy found it difficult to breathe. Every breath was accompanied by a sharp pain.

The rain and the cold did not seem to matter anymore, for he could not feel his body. He could not even think clearly. This 'couldn't care less' attitude was dangerous and he knew it. His little body would not stop shaking. Breathing in and out also proofed difficult, accompanied by little stabs every time he gasped for air.

He knew how dangerous the situation had become
If he wouldn't be able to find somewhere to shelter soon
this would do him in.

A dog was barking from somewhere close by, on
of those that usually had a chain on the end of its colla
otherwise it would have made mincemeat of anyon
passing by, including him. He had managed to avoid th
dog and finally arrived at the source of the red glow, righ
in the heart of the industrial area.

It must be early morning now, he thought.

He stopped and scanned the area.

It was riddled with furnaces of all shapes and sizes
In between plenty of old huts and storerooms, and h
could hear the sound of heavy hammers hitting the anvil
The alternating clonk of two hammers forging the stee
was louder than any storm. He could hear hardened stee
meeting glowing iron, forming it into a new shape, th
sparks rocketing towards the night sky and the wate
hissing as the iron entered the small cooling pool.

The boy carried on, dragging himself along som
dark path, aiming for an old barn with no light, seemingl
deserted and unused.

The doors were blocked by numerous pieces o
discarded machinery, empty barrels, rusty horseshoes an
even a broken carriage that leaned upright against th
barn wall. The boy decided to try his luck. Looking up
he had spotted a couple of dislodged planks, opening :
space big enough to slide through and get himself into th
dry. Summoning all of his remaining strength, he pulle
himself onto the wheel of the carriage, and then standin;

on the edge of the carriage frame, he hauled himself up and slid through the inviting gap like a wriggling eel.

Not able to find anything to support his feet, and also unable to see what was beneath him, he plucked up all his courage and let himself drop.

He felt his toes hitting something soft. Something that eventually engulfed him up to his knees. It made him sneeze, but he could not figure out what he had landed in.

As he tried to turn around, waiting for his tired eyes to adjust to the dim light of the room, he sank deeper into that strange material. Still unsure of his new surroundings, he stretched out his arms to stop himself from sinking any further.

His heart started beating faster and faster and he stopped moving. And as he stood there, listening to the rain playing its symphony against the tin roof, he felt something rising up around him. Something he had longed for ever since he had left the school.

Warmth.

Of course, the boy thought. *Straw.*

The way it rustles and pokes into my skin. The way it makes me sneeze. Now, as my blood and my senses are coming back to life, I can feel how it is gradually warming me up.

"Straw," he sighed, relieved that he had finally found somewhere to shelter. He felt his eyes welling up for just a moment, but he did not have the strength to cry. All he wanted was to be at peace.

He leaned forward and picked up enough of the yellow gold to free his chest and his legs. Next he stamped and pressed the straw down until he had created a surface

to lie on. He laid on his back and placed enough straw ove
his arms, legs and body so that only his head poked out.

Buried deeply in his pile of straw, he shivered fo
warmth until he finally felt his cold body had thawing out
and the warmth entering every inch of it. It did not tak
long for him to fall into a deep sleep.

To begin with, his little lips were still twitching
and his forehead crinkled due to the sort of bad dream
naturally encountered after a strenuous day. But soon
exhaustion took over and transported the boy to a plac
where there was little to worry about.

He did not notice how a whisper rang through the ai
from the other side of the barn. Nor did he notice the answe
accompanied by a sharp *psst*, and then it all went quiet.

Until the next day.

CHAPTER 9

Friends

As long as we stick together, we
can master every hurdle

"Astray," a child's voice sounded. "How did he get in here?"

More than a dozen pairs of eyes stared down onto the sleeping bundle.

"Via the carriage," someone answered, "just like we do."

"What are we going to do?"

All eyes wandered over to a young girl with shaggy braided hair leaning against a wall.

"Let him sleep. He's not going to harm us," she answered, reaching for the gap and pulling herself up like she had done so many times before. She looked up at the cloudy sky, then into the deep puddles the storm had left on the ground. *There is more rain to come, at least this morning,* she thought "Is it bad?" her little brother asked from below.

The girl sat on the ledge of some broken planks.

"Bad enough," she said. "People will not venture far today. It is going to be a meagre day."

The children around her nodded.

"Well," the girl said. "We don't have much choice if we want to eat. Whose turn is it to take the shoeshine box?"

Two of the strapping lads lifted their hands, and someone pushed the box towards them.

"And who is asking for handouts today, preferably down by the cathedral and the shops?"

Three children, beakers in hand, stepped forward.

"Good," said the girl. "The others will search the alleys leading from the marketplace for food. Pick up anything that looks edible or has been discarded by the market traders."

She glanced at the group once more and looked at its smallest member, a little orphaned boy whom they had only picked up a couple of weeks ago.

"You will stay here and look after this one," she said and pointed at the sleeping boy. "He will require our help and we might even need his."

She turned and clambered further up onto the roof. The other children followed her and left the barn, all heading on their merry way.

It was late evening before they reappeared, soaked through to the skin and famished. The girl was last. She did not enter the refuge until she was absolutely certain that no one had followed them.

The boy sat on his bed of straw, rubbing the sleep out of his eyes. He had slept for most of the day. His little overseer greeted the girl with a warm smile. She passed him a piece of bread out of her pocket and stroked his head.

"And? Have you put him in the picture?" she asked.

"He's only just woken up," the little overseer giggled.

"Well, best you two follow me then."

They worked their way through the thick straw until they arrived in the farthest corner of the barn. The area was dimly lit with planks arranged to act as seating, and nearly all the places had already been taken. The girl gestured the two boys to sit down and placed her apron in the middle of the floor. One by one, the children placed the yield of the day on the apron. Bunches of carrots, a bag full of cucumbers, several slices of bread, all in all equating to about two loaves, pears, a block of butter and a hat full of nuts. The collection tins were tipped out and counted. Twenty-six pennies altogether. A miserable day.

At least there is enough to feed us all, the girl thought. *We just have to hope that the winter will not arrive too early, for we will still need a few coats, socks and two pairs of shoes.*

She looked at the boy. *Three pairs of shoes,* she thought, and emptied today's pennies into a little pouch she wore around her neck. She split the food into the number of mouths that needed filling and spoke. "As long as we stick together, we can master every hurdle."

The kids raised their heads and repeated. "As long as we stick together, we can master every hurdle."

Suddenly, the boy realised who he was dealing with.

"You? You two?" he said, recognising them as the

couple that had helped him get into the school.

"Hey, stray," answered the girl, "how was life in school?"

"I…" the boy cleared his throat. "I… still need to.. thank you."

"There is still plenty of time for that," said the girl. "You should eat first." She smiled and as the boy looked into the circle, he recognised her—eagerly munching—little brother among the crowd.

I had hoped that I would see them again, he thought. *But never believed it would actually happen. Not after spending such a long time with my head in the books.*

He cleared his throat once again and wolfed his slice of bread down. Everyone remained silent, with their bellies full tiredness set in quickly and thus, going off in pairs or in groups of three they headed to their sleeping places. They lay tightly huddled, one next to another, deeply snuggled down into the straw, keeping warm during the night.

Silence fell over the barn. Apart from the girl.

She had taken the boy aside so as not to disturb the others. They were lying that close that the tips of their noses were almost touching.

Whispering away, she told him all about their little group. How they had all left home for one reason or another. Either because there was nobody left to look after them, or because they had to take their future into their own hands for whatever reason.

They all stemmed from the valleys outside of the town, those same valleys where the ruthless tycoon was going about his ruthless business. Where he had bough farm after farm, land after land and forced the residents to work for him, earning themselves a pittance, whilst he himself was filling his coffers, supported by a network of equally ruthless traders.

They did not care where their goods came from or under what conditions they were produced, as long as they received their share. A never-ending circle that hit those who tried to preserve their independence.

"There will be more children," the girl whispered. "The hunger will drive them into the town."

She told him about the other groups, one hiding by the harbour, another on the outskirts of the labourers' district, and one more in another suburb. They all lived from hand to mouth and whatever they found to make ends meet, would get less with each new arrival.

"One day there will not be enough to go round anymore," she said. "The day will come when no one wants their shoes cleaned anymore. And we have nothing else to offer…"

"To offer?" whispered the boy.

"To offer to the grown-ups. In exchange for something only they have enough of."

The boy rolled his eyes wondering what she meant and at the same time pushed a piece of straw aside that was poking in his cheek. The straw rustled and the girl grabbed his hand and pushed it quietly to the floor.

"Quiet," she said.

There was thick fog outside and the barn was as dark as a cloudy night during winter solstice. The girl could not see the boy opposite her, but she could feel that he was thinking about what she had just said and she started to make plans.

"We have nothing to offer?" whispered the boy. No exactly a question, but the beginning of a new thought, fo the old one was not worth pursuing further.

"*We* have nothing," said the girl, and gently presse his hand like his mother used to, and then added, "but *yo* have."

"Me?"

"Tell me about the school," she asked, "but quietly."

There was a tone of excitement in her voice and th boy knew that it was his turn now, so he started speakin about his experience. He spoke about conformity and o how everyone did alike, and about reading, writing an doing maths and all the other magical things that wer written down in books for everybody to learn. Food fo thought and dreams, so powerful that you would thin about it first thing in the morning and last thing at night

He spoke about his difficulties learning until he wa able to read properly, and how the librarian had taken he time and patiently taught him what he needed to know How success had finally arrived and how he had becom a bit of a bookworm, how he had fed his hunger fo knowledge, until the day when luck had left him, and he' found himself on the streets once more.

The boy stopped for he could feel her shallov breathing next to his cheek. He realised there was nothing more to talk about that night.

She is asleep, he thought, and closed his eyes.

But the girl was still wide awake. Like an owl, she le

her eyes wander through the darkness.

She touched the pouch around her neck, weighing it up with her hand to see if there was enough.

Hopefully, there is, she thought.

"It will have to be!" You could hear her gentle voice after a while in an otherwise silent barn. "It will have to be."

CHAPTER 10

Kindness

Be kind, don't judge, you don't know their story

The day began with a loud bang. The whole industria quarter erupted as a hot flow of lava poured int a water butt, bursting pipes to a length of abou four hundred feet. The children in the barn woke up ii an instant. They could hear the screaming outside, th sounds of heavy boots stomping on the floor and throug the alleys, taking over.

Amongst it all, the sound of sirens and neighin horses as they pulled the fire carriages full of water to th scene of the incident.

The children had quickly overcome the initial shock These sorts of accidents happened regularly, sometime caused by one of the workers, other times by the fatigue machinery coming into contact with glowing red-hot iron

The girl, however, wanted to seize the moment. She quickly distributed the day's chores to her charges and then climbed out through the rafters.

"Follow me, scruff bag," she said to the boy, and slid down the planked wall onto the upturned carriage. By the time the boy had pushed his head through the rafters, the girl was already well on her way. He found her waiting for him at the corner of a factory. He hurried and they soon left the industrial quarter behind. By the time the sun had set on the horizon, they had already crossed the little swing bridge over the river. As they hurried through the streets and alleys, the town was beginning to come to life. Windows opened, and that strange morning buzz the boy had already experienced down in the suburb started to appear. He knew what was about to come.

The two were running through the streets lined with the shoe box houses, their walls as grey as ash. As the first doors opened, members of the workforce entered the road, clutching a briefcase in the right hand and a cigarette in the left or vice versa.

They had black shadows under their eyes, their shoulders hanging just like puppets. The boy had no problems dodging their steady flow, but he did have problems keeping up with the girl.

Being away from home has softened me, he thought. *My legs are giving up again, and my lungs too. On top of that I have no idea where we are heading or how far we still have to go.*

"It is not your legs that have given up. You have been cheating them," I reminded him. "And yourself!"

"Cheating myself?" he wheezed.

"The five essences for a healthy life. The most important treasures. Do you remember?"

The boy had trouble remembering. Then the girl suddenly stopped They had entered the main shopping precinct. He managed to catch up with her and stopped right next to her.

Number four, he thought.

"I remember now," he said, and the girl looked at him a bit puzzled.

"This way," she said without showing any sign of tiredness. They followed the path down a horseshoe-shaped alley, leaving the windowless wall to the left behind them and then turning right they finally arrived at a staircase where they turned off once more.

The town had opened up into a great expanse and the girl had finally stopped running. Instead she scanned all the windows until she stopped outside one particular one. As she did so, she wet her hand in a puddle and ran it over her hair to smooth it down. Next she pulled her dress into place and checked her reflection in one of the shop windows. Noticing the dirt on her face, she scooped up more water out of another nearby puddle and washed the dirt off herself.

Finally ready to do what she intended, she nodded at the boy and they both entered the shop.

As they went through the door, a bell rang announcing the visitors, which caused a well-dressed man to turn around in joyful anticipation of receiving his first customers of the day.

"My mother sent me," the girl said.

Not waiting for an answer, she took the pouch from her neck and jangled the coins. She pointed at the boy and said, "Our new groom. He needs new clothes."

A man in a fine suit, who was a tailor, understood and led the pair into a side room.

"If Miss would like to look through the rails for something that suits," he said, and returned to the entrance.

The girl knew exactly what she wanted the boy to have. It didn't take long before she had found a pair of long trousers, a shirt and a thick coat. Then she walked over to one side of the room and pulled a curtain aside. The boy could not quite comprehend the nature of all of this, but he understood that his leather shorts and linen shirt would not get him through the winter. A winter without a stove would be just as hard in the flatlands as in the mountains. So, he did as requested and stepped behind the curtain to change his clothing. It pained him to see his old clothes in a heap on the floor, frayed and dirty. He could see a piece of himself lying there.

Why is it always so difficult to part with the old? It does not make sense. I should be glad that I am getting something new, he thought. *Just like a bee happy to be landing on the first spring flowers, or that time when the weaver woman presented me with that linen shirt. And then when the shirt got torn to shreds as they ran me down. The pain, the loss of it at the time may have been short and sharp, nothing like now, where I feel I am leaving part of me behind.*

"Don't even think about it," I said. "Not now, not ever. Don't be sad about things past."

And it was precisely then that the boy decided to leave the tailor's shop without his old trousers and shirt and never to waste another thought over them.

"Something is missing," the girl said, mustering him from top to bottom.

The boy in front of her looked good in his new attire. But not good enough, at least not for her liking. She buried her hands in her pockets as she kept inspecting him over and over. She looked over to the rails and shelves for inspiration and suddenly... "Of course," she remarked.

She picked up a flat cap and placed it on the boy's head. *Yes, that's it,* she thought. *That is exactly it.*

He looks like a different person. The others will hardly recognise him. But enough now, I have spent too much already. I am spending the coins before we have even earned them, and money is hard enough to come by as it is.

They paid up and walked into another lane, where they stopped outside a cobbler's shop to buy a good pair of shoes and socks for him. The girl said that all the necessary preparations were now dealt with. She said this almost in passing, as if she was ticking another item off her agenda.

In the meantime, the town had come to life, just the way the girl had planned. She had stopped rushing around. There was no need anymore. Their destination was just a stone's throw away or at least it would have been if they had been able to fly over the houses blocking the way.

Behind the row of tradesmen's houses gleamed a glass palace. Little inclusions in the windows sparkled in the sunlight like stars in the night. The morning dew was still burning off in the sunshine, the vapour steaming toward

the sky, only interrupted by a pair of passing doves h
towards the marketplace in search of a crumb or two.

As they approached the banking district, the boy sensed something magical. Not only that the pavements were wider and framed with bollards set at a regular distance, but there were also little beds of flowers and grass on the forecourt. Trees, adorning their autumn leaves, held their crowns up majestically toward the sky. They represented a certain power, almost like everything in this street. Even the people were different. They were in no rush, standing in small groups of two or three, holding discreet conversation about the weather, business and the finer things in life. They either owned a lot of one thing or wanted more of another, and the deal was usually done amongst each other outside on the pavement, or inside one of the cafes lining the street that would have been inviting even without the sheepskin pelts draped over the seats.

We are finally here, thought the girl.

They stopped outside the entrance of the modest ten-storey-high glass tower, which was outdone in its height by some of the surrounding ones that were even higher, wider and longer.

"We are here because of the sign," she reminded herself, and she pointed at a sign hanging next to the entrance and asked the boy, seemingly in awe of the gleaming building and all the well-dressed people, to read to her what was written there.

I, myself noticed that no one seemed to take much notice of the sign. People were far too well off to care about a sign like this.

The girl had watched the previous evening how an old man had hung the sign in the window by the entrance. At the same time, she had also witnessed a young man being chased out of the building. He had worn a flat cap and the whole incident had left her curious. All this had happened whilst she was on her way back to the refuge hungry and tired.

"Messenger wanted," the boy said.

A well-dressed man, standing a little further away pricked his ears up. He pretended to listen to his counterpart, but in reality he was much more focused on the pair of young children in front of the sign. He wondered if they were brother and sister, but quickly dismissed that thought, for the girl was not as well dressed as the boy.

"I thought so," the girl whispered.

"And below? What's written below?"

She pointed to the small print, her finger hovering impatiently over the words like a piano player's finger hovering above the right key.

The boy read aloud:

"One shilling a day."

There was more. The boy continued reading and the girl listened intently, one finger under her chin as though she was thinking, and then her eyes started gleaming and the boy understood.

Impossible, he thought. *No one will employ a scruff bag like me. Albeit a well-dressed scruff bag. But the cloth will not disguise where I have come from and what I have been through. I would be much better off cleaning shoes or sitting in a corner with a beaker in my hand, not speaking to anyone*

That way, I can also keep my pride, for if someone gives me a coin, they would do this of their own free will and not because of my begging. And I would not be refused so I could keep my self-esteem.

Yes, he thought, *I would rather be out on the streets, searching and collecting discarded items than being the lowest of the low in these surroundings of grandeur. That's impossible.*

"Nothing is impossible," said I. "Did I tell you that no one is more familiar with all the excuses under the sun, than I? Excuses that multiply like flies that later become pests. Ask a cuckoo, a cat or even a snake about the safety of a nest or a den, and they will laugh at the absurdity and put you into the picture. And not to forget the headmaster; he did not like anyone nesting under his roof now, did he?"

I continued bashing on at the boy until he shut up. But the girl, the girl kept on smiling.

And just as the whole situation could not get any worse, there it was again. My old adversary, the toad.

It had been there all this time, albeit subdued, but lingering in the background, still licking its wounds from the last defeat. It had not forgotten how badly it had been treated by the well, outside the place of knowledge, that day when it tripped over its own tongue, hitting the floor and rushing away like a thug. Now it was time to get its own back, and it would have been an easy game, for everyone knows how easy it is to catch someone off guard.

And I knew it too. The toad would thrive under the elixir of weakness. It would take full advantage of the situation.

I watched how the boy twitched nervously. How the

bony, three-fingered claws came out from behind the sign and started reaching to the front. Reaching for the boy Slowly but surely, the slimy head peered from underneath the bottom corner of the sign and the boy stared straight into the elliptical red eyes of the toad, making his stomach turn. He started shaking and the toad blinked expectantly making the boy shake even more.

It is all too much, he thought. *This place, the splendour the new clothes, owing the girl.*

The expectations the boy felt he had to live up to were far too much. Suddenly, the girl said. "What's the matter? What is the matter with you?"

The boy did not hear her.

His stare was fixated at the sign, the toad's eyes and the entrance hall in the background.

The toad had already opened its mouth and it sucked in the fear. It inflated itself with every gulp it took in, growing as big as possible. Ready for things to come Slowly but surely. Slime dripping out of every pore.

It was sweating in excitement.

I was about to summon all my friends, helpers and protectors, and everyone and everything to come to the aid of my little friend.

Not just Luck and Fate as they seemed to be absent right now. But everyone remained quiet, and by now the girl had stopped smiling.

"What is the matter with you?" she asked again, this time a bit louder.

The boy thought about running away, or hiding but before the thought could materialise into any action voice came from behind.

"Fancy a swap?"

The girl took a fright and stepped aside, only to see that the question had been addressed to the boy.

"Are you here to swap?" the man said, wondering why this well-dressed boy was fixated to the corner of the sign. This boy had read the writing on the sign beautifully and fluently, better than some adults would have been able to. And it was exactly that which had attracted the man.

He had not only looked at the girl's beaming face but also seen the boy's upset. And that's how he knew he had to step in. He left his business partners behind and walked over to the boy, but the boy did not acknowledge him.

I am not sure whether his fear would not let him or whether he hadn't even noticed the man.

There is only one thing for it, the man thought, and stepped between the boy and the sign.

He bent down and smiled at the boy. The toad stopped in its tracks, cursing the strong back that suddenly stood in its way.

It had inflated itself with all its might and now, but without being able to influence the boy any further, it was unable to act. It shook itself, gasped for air, shook itself again—this time much harder—and then it suddenly burst. *Gone*—with a loud bang.

This was the moment the boy broke out of his daydream. He looked straight into the two kind eyes and suddenly noticed the well-formed, albeit thin mouth, that spoke in a kind manner. "You are here to swap, aren't you?"

The boy shook himself, almost as if he wanted to get

rid of the last of the toad. It seemed to help; he regained composure and now he finally looked at the man in front of him, at his pinstriped suit, the broad shoulders dressed in a tailored jacket with a waistcoat of the same material and of course, the golden watchchain. The man was in no rush.

"Today is a good day," he said.

"A good day?" the boy enquired.

"For a swap."

"For a swap?"

"Yes," said the man. "What you possess already for what you want. You see, the whole of life is all about swapping. We are constantly swapping one thing for another, and at the end of our days, we find out who was good at swapping and who wasn't."

The boy was curious.

"Can you offer me what is wanted on the sign?" asked the man. He knew that someone who could read that well would also be able to write and do maths. And at that early age, that was special, very special indeed.

"Yes," the boy answered, and grinned. "I have been to the place where knowledge lives and had a teacher just for myself. I can offer what's wanted here."

The man stood up and looked at his pocket watch. Then he nodded.

"Then please follow me," he said. "Follow me and we will make our first swap. Your knowledge and your time for a shilling a day."

The boy looked over to the girl, who took his hand and squeezed it gently. "You go," she said, and started beaming again. She was happy, happy for him, for her and for all her charges.

Today is a good day, she thought. It may have started with a bang, but then hope took over.

I watched the boy as he followed the man through the splendid entrance of the bank. Everyone seemed to know the man, for they all stopped and bowed and spoke to him with great respect. Heavy oak desks and chairs filled the big booking hall. He climbed the marble staircase, where portraits were lining either side of the wall. Their subjects all had the same thin mouth, and all were portrayed in a fashion that indicated they had once been of much importance. The first floor and all the others above were a mirror image of the booking hall. People wore suits and carried notes to and fro and shouted numbers and figures at each other, almost as if using a code rather than the spoken word.

"They are swapping too," the man explained, and winked at the boy.

"And the better they are, the richer they become and so do I."

"But…" and he put his hand on his chest, just where the heart is located. "But money is not the most important thing in life. It is as I said. We will find out at the end of our days, who was good at swapping and who was not."

CHAPTER 11

Growth

Every day in life, good or bad, is a day of growth

Grow or go, grow or go, grow or go…

The boy opened his eyes and the echo in his head instantly stopped. It was dark and cold outside. He lifted his legs up and felt the straw nestle. Another couple of minutes and he would have to get up and start the long walk to the banking district. He usually got up earlier than all the others, giving him time to think or just to lay in the straw for another moment, listening to the breathing of his friends with whom he had shared everything, and who had become as close to him as his family.

They had managed to survive the winter despite all the odds life sometimes throws at people. It had certainly made them stronger.

The boy brought home six shillings a week, and even on Sundays, his well-deserved day off, he would not sit back and always help wherever he could. The girl did not tolerate laziness anyway, and even if she did, it was an unwritten law amongst all the children not to stop until all the chores were done.

And it had paid off.

Well before the first snowflakes sprinkled from the sky, they had already stopped being cold.

And not just because it was a mild winter, but because they had earned enough money for everyone to call a pair of boots and a thick winter coat their own. And that together with a pair of gloves, a scarf and a bobble hat.

Food was plentiful and the children had perked up and did what all children did. They jumped and played and climbed about in their den, so loud at times that the girl had to call them to order. Until now, they had not been found out and she hoped that they would be able to remain in their barn for a long time to come.

The straw nestled and the boy realised that it was time to get up. He freed himself from his nest and put on the coat that he used every night to cover himself.

He felt for his flat cap that usually resided in the right coat pocket and pulled it over his frizzy hair. Then he took his scarf out of his left-hand pocket and wrapped it round his neck three times, pushing both ends into the coat opening. He put on his boots and pulled the laces tight. His toes had gotten used to the warmth and comfort the boots offered, and the cold, dirty cobblestones were long forgotten. Last but not least, he bent down to the

girl and put his hand very gently on her back, just on he
shoulder blades, only for a brief moment and then he wa
on his merry way.

He climbed through the rafters, down the carriag
and off he went, the ground crunching under his feet. H
liked the icy cold—how the water froze in his nose befor
it could form a drip that would later drop down. And
even more so, he liked the warm clothes that gave him th
feeling that he was well prepared for anything this ice-col
winter might throw at him.

Accompanied by the sound of hammers crashin
down on anvils, the boy arrived at the river crossing. H
knew every shortcut and every safe passage. It helped hin
to remain undetected by the workmen, the guard dogs and
the carriages toing and froing their heavy loads of iron and
ore to the docking stations by the river.

It was only after he had crossed the river that h
blended into the masses rushing to work. He arrived at th
bank just after sunrise every morning.

His boss, the owner of the bank and of many othe
glass palaces in this town—they all just called him *Th*
Banker—did not arrive until shortly after midday. His fac
looked paler than usual, and the boy started wondering i
everything was in order.

The banker set eyes on the boy just as he was carryin
a pile of notes and papers under his arm. He asked hin
to follow him into his office, and minutes later, they sa
in comfortable chairs. The banker had sent for two cup
of tea, some caramelised sugar and a plate full of hand
decorated biscuits, which he pushed towards the bo

without helping himself.

"How long have you been working for me now?" he asked.

The boy took his fingers to help with the counting and answered, "One hundred and twenty-six days, sir."

"Are you sure?"

The boy went quiet.

"And how much have you earned so far in your time with me?"

"One hundred and eight shillings." The boy did not hesitate. "That does not include today."

"A little fortune. Am I right?"

The boy nodded.

"But you don't spend it on yourself, am I right?"

The boy nodded.

"See…" The banker leaned forward and took one of the biscuits and dunked it quickly into his unsweetened tea "…there was once a time, when a man whose name I carry…" He looked up at one of the life-sized portraits to his right before he continued. "There was once a man, who was very much like you, and this man founded all of this."

The butler entered to pour more tea. The boy seized the moment and took a sweet.

"He has immortalized himself," said the banker, "He has immortalized himself and I am his custodian."

"A good swap?"

"I think so," answered the boy.

The banker smiled.

"You think so?"

If only he knew how much I envy him, thought the pale man. *Envy him for what he has.*

"I have made a thousand swaps, more even, but have not always got it right, because I have been driven by greed and the greed has blinded me. It has almost made me addicted. One glass palace, the one my father built, would have been enough, but I wanted more, another and another and now I am like all the others that cannot get enough to fill their inner void."

The boy felt a certain sadness rising within this incredibly rich man who had learned to mask his empty heart with a smile. The butler entered once more and announced in a polite but stern voice, that an important customer was waiting in the salon.

It took the banker a moment before he reluctantly got off his chair. Reluctant, because he knew that the next hour would be a wasted one, but also unavoidable. So he took a folder, opened the page marked and made some notes on a piece of paper. He closed the folder, nodded at the butler and asked him to show the customer in.

Turning towards the boy, he said. "Take the rest of the day off and think about a swap that is worth it."

The boy grabbed his flat cap and left.

Just before he got to the door, he heard a command. "Hey, catch."

The banker threw a coin high into the air and the boy instinctively jumped up to grab it. Once safely in his hand, the boy laughed and so did the banker, happy that his little trick had brought some joy to them both.

The boy stashed the coin safely in his pocket, waved

farewell and smiled happily, but as he turned around, he bumped into a monstrous gut.

"You rascal, watch where you are going," a sharp voice groaned.

A bundle of memorandums and letters fell to the floor and created chaos. The boy went to gather them, but a rough hand pushed him aside and the smell of tobacco got under his nose.

"Mon dieu," the butler cried, and quicky rushed across to pick the notes off the floor.

"A misfortune," he cried. "Please accept our apologies, dear sir."

"Apologies?" sounded the voice. "I am not here to be gracious. I am here to do business."

The banker, who had witnessed the incident, said nothing. He merely raised his eyebrows and then asked himself if his customer was getting fatter and fatter with each visit, and whether he would still fit into the chair.

The chair creaked loudly under the weight pressed upon it, but it held. Just. A large fat hand wandered into the pocket of the frock coat and pulled something out. Something that gleamed. At that very moment, the boy looked up from the floor and it was as if a lance had stabbed him straight into the heart. His little hands bunched up into tight little fists.

Its him, thought the boy. *The tycoon. The enemy of everyone and everything I hold dear. He has destroyed my world and now he is here, being his opinionated self, and he behaves as if nothing has happened. He does not care who or what he destroys, and he will not stop, not ever, unless someone puts a stop to him.*

It was only the butler who noticed the inner upheava in the normally quiet child, the mixture of anger and th longing of revenge, and how wrong it all felt.

"Come, child," he said quietly, bowing to both mer who no longer took any notice of him; they had alread engaged into a conversation. Closing the door behinc them, the butler pointed to a stool and motioned for th boy to sit down and sort his papers, which he duly did. H did it because his instincts told him to, and also becaus he could hear the annoyingly loud voice of the tycoon. H needed to know what was going on behind that door.

"Sir, your calculations are flawed," he heard th banker say.

Something banged on the table. Twice. It may hav been folders but may also have been fists. Fists that deniec the making of mistakes.

"I have never ever made a mistake in my life," th tycoon thundered. "Look at my turnover of goods. Peopl are snatching the stuff from my hands."

"Yes, but every sack of flour and every pound o cheese you sell, you pay over the odds for."

"Not for long," ensured the tycoon, sniggerin; cynically at the same time.

"The coming spring will finally bring the profits desire, and if I have to squeeze them out of the farmers— and squeeze them I will, trust me. Next spring there will b enough to meet your monthly payments."

"And the payments from last year?" the banker askec

"Yes, and the payments from last year."

"And the payments from the year before?"

"You…" the tycoon thundered, and the boy could feel the hatred through the door, spreading right through the atmosphere of the glass palace like a foul stench.

"Careful, you. If you let me go under, I will take you with me."

The tycoon raised his mighty body and looked into the direction of the portraits.

"I am sure you will not want to disappoint," he said, grinning cynically.

The banker gasped for air. Something in him broke and for a moment or so, he thought that this would be the end. But then he closed his eyes and sank back into the soft leather of his chair.

He was sick of the arguments.

Arguments about money. Sick of having to be rude and scurrilous and sometimes even cunning. For deep down inside, he was disgusted about all the bad things money entailed.

Take a deep breath, he thought. *Take a deep breath and let all the bad feelings out until the pain in your chest disappears. That is the only swap you can do now. The only swap that is worth its while.*

The banker took his time. He slowly opened his eyes and it seemed as if he was paying the man opposite him full attention, but he wasn't. He was concentrating wholly on the pain and could feel it disappearing.

The tycoon, however, was about to embark on a rage and a rant. The farmers had to be forced to their luck because they were uneducated and lacking ambition. And

he alone knew what would be good for them. And tha
would be a life in servitude, a life where thinking woulc
be done for them and thus it would steer their life into
something useful.

He spoke of quotas and of low wages, starting a
soon as he had harassed even the last farmer into servitude
when all the valleys and all the folk would depend on him

"I will be raking it in. I will be raking in a fortune."

He took a cigar from the golden case and lit up
Smoke rose towards the ceiling and hung around the room

The banker did not like the smell of tobacco and
turned to open a window. He let in the cold dry air, and i
smelled like the end of winter. The clouds in the sky ha
been lifted by the lunchtime sun, leaving just a few stripe
on the horizon.

But apart from that, the sky presented itself in the
brightest of blue. Crowds of people moved onto the
pavements to soak up the sunshine. The banker suddenl
felt adventurous.

I'll request a carriage, he thought. *A trip to the meadou
or even farther, where no one is around, and no one can spoi
my day. There, I will sit and look into the sky and listen to th
wind blowing through the grass. And I will think of nothin
else until the evening.*

The banker suddenly felt content with himself and
everything around him.

"I am giving you one more reprieve," he said.

The tycoon nodded in satisfaction.

"I will give you until the summer solstice."

The tycoon stared at him in disbelief.

"What? So soon?"

"Yes," answered the banker and walked towards the door without looking back. "And if you have not paid me by then, I will take possession of the warehouses, the factories, the mills and everything else I have financed so far. You have my word."

The tycoon erupted inside but remained silent.

He stubbed the cigar out and took a long look at the portrait. He thought of bad things, very bad things. Things that he would implement to secure his status at all costs. And he thought of his motto, deeply engraved into his heart, a heart that had long turned to stone or even worse, something dark and hard without a name. He whispered his motto to himself, over and over again.

It took a while for the butler to return. The banker had already left and was just turning into the street that housed the cathedral, heading east towards the meadows. He would not require the services of his right-hand man until the evening but had ordered him to escort the bothersome customer outside.

"Is there anything else I can help you with, dear sir?" asked the butler moments later.

He bowed to the man, hoping to ease his bad mood.

"My carriage," the other commanded. "Now!"

He rose, spat on the floor and stomped towards the staircase, not taking any notice of the boy nor the little old lady he ran into on the way out.

All he saw was an endless queue of ragged figures with shaven heads, how they worked the fields carrying heavy loads, and how some of them faltered under the strain of it all.

He felt good and knew that the vision before hi eyes would become reality. And that, and only that, woul occupy him over the coming weeks and months, for it wa the only way to earn the so badly needed monies he craved

I have heard enough, thought the boy. *Enough to kno what will happen to father, mother and my siblings, and no only them, but also the families of my friends.*

He handed the now sorted papers and notes over t the butler and bid him a polite farewell.

Time is running out, he thought, *and whilst time progressing, I cannot stay here and swap something that is no value to me anymore.*

And with this, he left the glass palace and wandere through the magnificent avenue, totally lost in his thoughts

"Now what will you do?" I asked.

The boy did not answer.

"Or more to the point, what can you do?"

The boy shook his head, walked over to a hedge an broke off a small twig. He stuck it in his mouth. The sma end started toing and froing as the boy continued walking He thought about the tycoon and of the time when he ha first set eyes on him. "Grow or go," the man had said an with that, events had unfolded that had turned out equa to a nightmare. *Grow or go. That is the fate we all have t face if we do not fend for ourselves and grow until we are bi enough to sort out our own affairs.*

But how can a child defend himself with one shillin in his pocket that will soon be swapped for bread? Ho can someone who has to seek shelter in a barn, so as not t freeze to death, defend himself even if he wanted to?

"You are wrong," I said. I had seen plenty of deficiencies in this world, but I had also seen enough people far too blind to notice all the things of which they had plenty. So I explained to him that he was as strong and healthy as he could ever be, and that this was his greatest asset.

The moving of the twig halted, only to start again. This time, the tip moved quicker than ever before. The boy was thinking about one thing in particular.

"And do not forget," I continued. "Time heals and takes away the misery. If you play it right, then one day, this whole matter will be a story you will reminisce about with your children."

The boy had come to rest on one of the bollards. It was lunchtime and the street was busy with people, like a colony of ants going about their daily chores.

The sun shone on heads and warmed shoulders and the boy too felt the warmth under his winter coat. Not long until spring now. The buds on the trees may still be asleep for now, but it would only take a week or so of good weather and they would awake to a new life.

People poured out of their glass palaces, stepped onto the streets with hungry stomachs and turned their pale winter faces towards the warming sun, closing their eyes in delight.

So many people, thought the boy. *So many amongst so many more. Is there anyone here who could stand up to the tycoon,* he wondered. And when? And how? How could it be done?

And as the tip of twig kept swinging to and fro, the visions in the boy's head became clearer and clearer. He would surround himself with more like-minded people. He thought about the girl and her brother for one, the little orphan and the strapping lads who were his friends.

And he saw the other hordes of nameless children scattered all over the town. Orphaned, unwanted, through no fault of their own, just unlucky because fate had wanted it.

Yes, thought the boy. *I am not alone. I might be poor but I am not alone, and I have learned a lot in this town, in this chapter of my life. I have learned from books and from people. I know enough to turn fate around. But one thing is still missing. One very important thing.*

A man walked past; his nose buried in a book. He crossed the street and stopped on the other side, leaning against a freshly planted tree.

The white pages of the book glistened in the midday sun as he stood there and read.

The boy removed the twig from his mouth. He was asking himself what story the stranger may be reading. There were many stories, and the boy himself had always liked the old fables from the old masters best. Those texts that would tell a lot in few words. And as he watched the man and the budding tree, he remembered the fable he had read on his last day in the library. The fable about the little oak tree. And here it is:

Once upon a time, there stood a little oak tree amongst a large untouched forest. All around it, big trees stretched their branches high into the sky and robbed the little oak of much needed light and rain.

The little oak endured its humble existence. No one took any notice of it. Especially not in the spring when everything around it aimed for growth and magnificence.

Until one day, when a strong hailstorm rained down onto the forest, taking away the leaves and fruits of the biggest and grandest trees. Shortly thereafter, another storm raged through the now bare trees with devastating effect. Those trees that did not blow over straight away, suffered broken branches under the force of nature.

Giant trees fell to the floor all around, but the little oak stood proud, waiting for nature's destruction to bring it to its timely end.

Three days later, when the sun shone through the clouds once more, there was nothing left of the once proud forest. The giant trees were torn and broken. Only the little oak stood proud in the midst of the field of devastation.

Suddenly, it found itself engulfed in sunlight and felt the moisture creeping from the soil into its roots. It did not hesitate to stretch itself out in all directions and bury its roots deeper into the ground.

Ten years later, the little oak had grown into a prosperous tree and a hundred years later, it finally stood proud like the king of trees in the naturally resurrected forest. Proud and beautiful like no other tree before.

And what do we learn from all of this? Well, let me tell you: Prepare yourself to weather the storm. And once you have overcome the storm, take your chances.

The boy remembered those words as if it was yesterday. He closed his eyes and bit down on the twig.

"Wait for the storm…" he mumbled, "wait for the storm and weather it."

The man on the other side closed his book and disappeared into a carriage. All that remained was the tree with the closed buds apart from one, right at the very top of the crown.

It had already opened, reaching for the sky. It was pure white, a vision of beauty to behold. The boy slid off the bollard and walked down the street. "My time will come after the storm," he mumbled to himself.

And it didn't take long for the storm to arrive. It came without warning, much to the shock and dismay of many people but brought with it the one thing the boy was still missing. And by the time the storm had passed, *everything* had changed.

CHAPTER 12

Changes

Grab them, when they come your way

A barge was heading for the quay, its hull high above the waterline. The crew stood lined up along the upper deck, their shaven heads deep between their shoulders. The dockworkers on the quay caught the mooring lines and started tugging the boat towards them to fasten the lines to the mooring bollards. The group that had been ordered to unload the boat and their men had been waiting all morning. They were astonished when the pale bargemen heaved themselves ashore only to disappear amongst the crowd. There was no load. Where was the ore? Another barge appeared on the horizon, floating towards the quay just as gently as the last.

This must be the one carrying the load, they agreed and prepared themselves once more, checking their baskets, the lifting gear and the wagons, the supervisors confirming their delivery notes a final time.

The second barge dropped off its crew who were just as grey, pale and despondent as the first. The third and fourth barges were the same, the only load on offer being misery. Life was difficult during this economic crises. Jobs were scarce and at the end of each day a lot of mouth went hungry. Come the evening, a few of them, the more persistent ones, were still present waiting at the quay hoping to snap up a load to transport. The rest had turned to the pubs to drown their sorrows, ever in the hope that things would return to normal the next day.

They toasted each other because they could not think of anything better to do, and they drank more than they should for fear of the unknown.

Outside, the usual constant glow of the furnace had dampened right down, at first hardly noticeable, but then after midnight, even the largest furnaces had been extinguished. Black smog was smouldering over the land and inside the pubs, the drunken and once cheering crowd had grown quiet and despondent.

"What now?" someone whispered. No one cared to remember where the question came from, but it took hold like a wildfire. The men could not wait any longer.

They congregated on the streets and headed toward the town. They appeared from all sides, the town was full of those who had lost their today and could not envisage their tomorrow. The only thing they had left was their drunken anger and in their rage, they left behind them a trail of devastation. It wasn't until the army was dispatched—

dispersing the masses—that the rebellion ended.

This first bad day was followed by a bad week and an even worse month. It became so bad that people would have preferred to erase it from their memories. But if you wanted to live, you would also have to live through the bad times. Those who could not adapt to these changing times chose to end their lives, many jumping into the ice cold river.

Others who were stronger, both mentally and physically, pulled themselves together and carried on. The boy was one of the latter and he took the girl by the hand.

"We cannot stay here," he said.

"Let us stay here," replied the girl. "Just for a few more days. It is safe here."

"It seems safe because the district has gone quiet," answered the boy. "Everything around us has gone dead on us. There is nothing here for us anymore."

The girl looked towards her group. The others sat in the straw, listening intently.

"Look," said the boy. "We have nothing coming in anymore, no funds and only very little food."

"And if you would look for employment… I am sure the banker would…"

"No one is employing anyone anymore, on the contrary. There are lots and lots of redundancies," the boy interrupted her.

"All those that need money, just as we need air to breathe, are on the streets protesting. And the rich, the very rich are holding their purse strings shut because the blood loss isn't done yet."

The girl nodded and the children in the corner lifted their heads in agreement.

"I am so worried about those fretting, those that are losing out," said the boy. "Today, they are holding up their signs looking for work and tomorrow they may well be looking for shelter. Next, they will tear open the entrance to the barn and will treat us like wolves treat a flock of sheep."

The girl put her arms around herself and swallowed heavily.

The boy had never been the intermediary of fate nor did he want to be. He simply tried to explain what he could see, what he had learned from watching people and how to read them. Their actions and their words had taught him caution.

"It is time to go," he said once more.

The group rose and stood in front of the boy.

"Then you will have to lead us now on," the little orphaned boy said, interrupting the silence.

The boy looked over to the girl.

"That he will," she said.

She felt how the load she had been carrying dropped off her shoulders and how her heart took a big leap, almost as if someone had removed the thorn of worry that came with the burden of care.

She stepped back and let the boy's voice fill the barn as he briefed his companions on the next act of their journey. It would take them to a very special place.

"Where is it you want to go? To the suburbs?"

The words came from an old wagon driver whose

loading bed was empty. He had already sold his good horse just before the prices had come down too far, and now he only had the old mare, whose joints were already worn out and whose old hooves held no more iron. The animal suffered under the strain, as the owner knew. Thus he tried to treat his beloved old mare gently and did not rush her one bit, for he knew how painful old worn-out bones could be. He wasn't the youngest anymore either.

The only thing they both longed for was a peaceful existence somewhere on the outskirts of town, a little shelter for him, a green meadow for her, somewhere they could spend their last days in peace.

We don't really want to walk that far, thought the boy, while he watched for a lift as they got to the road junction leading from the industrial quarter to the town. He had noticed the old carriage and thought that this old pair were about to take their last journey. A journey they would more than likely not ask to be paid for.

And he was right.

The coachman was far too tired to ask the boy any further questions, apart from one.

"What takes you there?"

"…creating a new home," the boy answered.

The man ignored the strange answer and nodded invitingly to the horde of children, signalling them to hop onto the cart. He didn't have to nod twice, They happily jumped on and their laughter awoke the last spirits within the old man and his mare, which just for a moment, caused them to forget their plight and sorrow.

The mare trotted as best she could and as the cold

wind reddened the cheeks of the children, they each felt a bit special.

They passed the houses looking like shoe boxes, th glass palaces and carried on along the mall and past th villas of the wealthy, through the triumphal arc and pas the old cathedral which was bathed in gentle light as if i was symbolising the stairway to heaven.

There was so much to see on this journey, not jus the glass palaces or the entry of the cathedral glowing i the sunlight, as if it were the entrance to eternity. The tree and alleys were without their usual hustle and bustle. Th children seated high up on the carriage were blinded by th glamour and did not notice the plight of the poor nor th stench rising from the gutter.

Instead, the bumpy ride had something invigoratin; about it, almost like standing under a cool waterfall on ; hot summer's afternoon, a relief from the usual gloom an despair of a typical day. The carriage stopped at the chose junction, the children climbed off, and following the boy headed towards the suburb. This time, he was comin; home, not leaving.

"I praise the Lord to find you so well," said the old weaver woman. "I have often thought about you and hav wished so much for your return."

The boy looked into her kind eyes. They coul easily have belonged to a child, the way they sparkled an gleamed behind those round glasses.

When did she pass?" he asked her, looking down a the little grave by the door. In the centre, a little cross mad from cut stone and to the left and the right, fresh flower marking her path over the rainbow bridge.

"Last winter," answered the weaver woman. "I have been…"

"Alone, since."

"Yes."

"Not anymore," said the boy, and in memory of little velvet paws who had kept watch over him during the night, he raised his voice and said, "I promise you wholeheartedly, weaver woman, that you will never ever be alone again, loneliness will never pain you ever again, for now you have us."

And his finger pointed to the cast-iron gate with the two turtle doves, where the children stood waiting. The girl headed the group together with her brother and the little orphaned boy on her arm. To the right, a group of boys whose coats still reached below their knees, and at the very back the strapping lads with their crooked flat caps.

The weaver woman started to cry tears of joy. She took the boy's arm, and he helped her shuffle down the stairs of her porch before he turned his head and whispered something into her ear.

She listened intently and every now and then, she nodded in agreement. Slowly but surely, the sad veil lifted off her face. She stood to welcome the children, asking each and every one for their name, where they came from and where they wanted to be. Each received a kiss on their forehead, and with each kiss a grain of sand fell back into her hourglass, giving her a new lease of life. She felt the energy of the young lives in front of her, and with it the will to try everything the boy had suggested.

"Of course I will give you all a home," she said "You have encountered a life of misery through no faul of your own. We will turn this misery into happines and your poverty will turn into abundance, you will see We will bundle our strength, for our community and fo everything we hold dear."

Hurrah, the children shouted, and it echoed off th walls of the suburb like a wakeup call.

Windows opened and people stretched their neck out to see what all the commotion was, only to see a grou of children dancing in the street. The weaver woman stoo in the middle of it all, her fingertips pressed to her lips an her hips swinging in time with the beat of everything tha went on around her. Suddenly, as if invisible hands wer leading them, the children broke the circle and walke hand in hand into the garden of the weaver woman's house

Soon a lot of noise could be heard, banging an sawing, sheep happily bleating, followed by the rattling o the loom. Footsteps could be heard all over the house an in the garden.

And behind the house, next to the giant trees, a bo shouted that he needed a saw.

A girl, basket in hand, rushed towards the raise vegetable beds while two boys brought water from th creek. The weaver woman opened the doors to the bar and pulled out an old handcart covered in dust and straw Two strapping lads set straight to work. They cleaned an dusted it off, repaired the spokes and restored it to its ol glory.

They loaded the water butts and pulled the car

towards the beds, giving the vegetable patch a much-needed watering.

The boy wanted the barn emptying, so the group focussed their attention on completing that next.

They heaped up the straw and neatly sorted the vast selection of tools—sickles, shovels, and digging forks—which now leaned against the outside of the barn wall. Multiple hands went to work, cleaning the tools and repairing what was needed. The weaver woman turned the grindstone and added sharpness where required.

Once done, they brought over planks and carried them along with everything else that would add a little comfort to the old barn. They worked away until each and every one of them had a bed, stacked three on top of each other, secured them tightly, with a ladder added to each set. At the end of each bed hung a suitable length of cloth, which, once pulled across, added the necessary darkness and privacy.

Soon after, each bunk was given a straw-filled mattress, two blankets and a pillow.

A whistle indicated that it was time for supper, but as soon as it was over, the banging and hammering started all over again and ran deep into the night, until no energy could be found.

The first week was hard and there was no bone that did not ache and no bruise that had not paid a price. The children slept deeper than they had ever slept before, awaking every morning with still aching bones, a feeling that did not even leave after their morning dip into the little creek just before they started work, and this feeling did not disappear until the first harvest.

But the constant pain had been worth it as the harvest was substantial. The children certainly understood the old saying, 'no pain, no gain'.

Every evening, they patted one another proudly on their shoulders, acknowledging their achievements. They motivated each other and vowed to achieve more than the miserable townsfolk, who had never been good at 'swapping' and were now drowning in their own misery.

"Today, we are still swapping our energy, our time and our knowledge for bread and shelter," the boy said to the others. "But tomorrow, we will be entering a new chapter."

He sent one set of his friends out to the nearest marketplaces to sell the excess cabbage, beetroot, herbs and other wares nature had to offer. For half of the usual price. Many of the towns folk were hungry and the crisis had left them short of money, They turned every penny and soon spotted the good deals that came from the children's baskets. It did not take long before they sold every item with their handcart and their baskets empty and their purses full.

Another group of children was sent out to search for the boy's teacher, for it was only the weaver woman and him that could read and that needed to change. It was time to exchange money and time for knowledge and educate all children, he knew that just as much as he knew how she longed to teach. His intent would suit both sides. Those who knew the town like the back of their hand went out looking for her until they found her in a carpenter's workshop, where she was sweeping floors in return for food and accommodation. But her intellect was starving and it did not take a lot to persuade her to follow the children to their new found paradise.

That very same evening the weaver woman welcomed her with the words: "Where have you been, beautiful soul? Hidden away in a workshop? I keep hearing only the best about you!"

The children stood and listened in delight. Their work was done and all that was left for today was to request their goodnight kiss and to return to their bunks to enter the world of dreams.

The old weaver woman took her time with what she had to say next. She sensed the shyness the young woman opposite her displayed, and it was never good to rush. You cannot build up trust in a hurry. So, she took a moment before she spoke in kind consideration.

"Have you managed to bury all the doubts, my dear?"

"Yes, I have," came the answer.

"Are you ready to shine brightly for those who need you the most?"

And she went on to say, "I promise I will be a dear friend to you. Always and forever. And, one day, when I am not so good anymore, I want you to take my place and take care of everything in this house with much love and kindness. As a weaver and as a mother. As a friend and as…"

"A teacher?"

"Yes, and that is how it shall be," said the weaver woman and opened her arms to welcome the young woman. A warm wind blew from the mountains and embraced both women, who became soul sisters that very night—a message from the forthcoming spring, it seemed. The weaver woman thought about the fresh green fields, the blossom and the crop that would start to grow very soon.

She thought about all the hard work that had to be put in, but it did not worry her.

Heart and mind were more than ready to work those hands and to do what needed to be done.

Spring was here and the storm had passed. It was their time and their chance, even if no one else outside of the house noticed. Or was it for the heck of it, that they decided to grab the upcoming way of life and get on with it.

CHAPTER 13

Teamwork

...is the name of the plan

"Pull it and secure it tightly," the boy shouted. "Higher, higher! A little bit more."

The day was still young and the morning cool, the task in hand was hard but well worth it. Working conditions were ideal for what they intended to do. They raised the tarpaulin between four birch trees until it came to rest with only a slight angle to the back. They wrapped the rope ends around the trees a couple of times and secured each rope with a half hitch knot.

The tarpaulin was made from the finest sailing cloth, an old sail in fact, one not needed anymore. The weaver woman had swapped it for a basket of her finest vegetables, and in with the deal came four long ropes. If you had food in abundance, you could swap it for almost anything during these harsh times, and that was exactly what they did. Half a dozen long benches, a blackboard, a few school desks, two boxes full of chalk and reams of light paper. Everything you needed to build your own school.

The townspeople had learned to show the weaver woman the necessary respect, especially now they needed her. They often formed long queues underneath the turtle doves in order to swap one or two unwanted things from better days for a delicacy fresh from the garden. Before too long, the rumour mill started, tales of a classroom under the sky. Of a young miss who did not need a rule to educate but turned each lesson into child's play. There were tales about her painting the words as well as writing them, and her speaking of a world outside of the town.

There were anecdotes about carts driven by adults but directed by children, heading to town fully laden with the bestest produce and often returning with a horde of scruffy looking children. But within a week under the watchful eye of the weaver woman they looked just as well suited and booted and were just as polite as the other children under her care.

People were astonished, secretly questioning where everything was coming from—how it was possible to feed all these hungry mouths and still have enough to sell to the neighbours, the traders, and the needy.

And the quality…

How could the quality be a thousand times better than anything anybody had ever tasted or laid eyes on and on top of that for half the price? It was only the bird who witnessed the long rows of vegetables lining the black soil all the way up to the edge of the forest. And it was only the birds who saw the chickens happily scratching for food from the nutritious gardens, the sheep with their little lambs leaping in the field, the rows of berries, the acres of winter hard wheat stalks that stretched their heads towards the sun. The fruit trees standing in full blossom and the mighty trees—chestnut, birch, oak, and ash—sheltering the little colony from unwelcome looks. Only the birds could see this green enclave with its clear stream of water and the flower beds, where they would stop over to rest, sing, and mate until the sun went down.

The birds saw the enclave in all its glory. The children, however, stood right in the middle and wiped the beads of sweat from their foreheads.

Including the boy.

He looked at his dirty hands, the thick skin and the blisters he had accumulated from the heavy work, and when he made them into little fists he could feel the hard skin digging into his palms.

How soft they once were, he thought. *In those days when I was still putting pen to paper. Now I have exchanged the pen for a spade, a shovel or a saw, and the hard labour is stamped onto my hands.*

Wonder what else can be read from those hands? Some say the future. Is that true?

Hopefully not, he thought, and wiped the dirt on his trouser legs.

Further to the north of the town, right on the edge of the labourer's district and in the port, they were also thinking about the future. "We have no future," complained the scruff bags. "Not here. But there is a futur about a day's walk away."

It sounded like a plan and they upped sticks an made their way towards the promised land. A land wher children looked after children, where there was no hunge and where they could be part of something big. Word ha got out that there was no judgement there, no differenc between rich and poor, good and bad, and other thing that would describe people in one way or the other.

By the time the tycoon heard all this, he was alread in dire straits. He could sense the danger and suddenl understood why his produce, coming from the valley remained unsold. He summoned his servant and sent hin to explore. When the servant returned, he confirmed th suspicions and described in much detail the goings on in the suburb.

The tycoon started ranting and raving. He almos burst with rage. He could not stand the thought of th townspeople queueing elsewhere, and if he could hav done, he would have put a stop to it straight away.

A green island, right on the outskirts of the town where everything was a-plenty. *I will have to wipe it off th map,* he thought, *or better still, I will take it over, like I hav taken over the valleys.*

"Who owns it? the servant was asked.

"Children, it seems," came the answer. With it, th servant only just managed to duck out of the way of a ju flying towards him before it crashed against the wall an burst into thousands of little pieces.

"Children!" screamed the tycoon. "I have bee

outwitted by children? That I will go and see for myself."

The servant felt strangely intimidated. He would have made a run for it if it weren't for the fact that his master had a certain hold over him. Thus, before too long, he sat opposite his master in his master's carriage, drawn by six fresh horses charging towards the suburb. On the front seat of the coach sat two of the master's thugs, fists as big and as hard as bricks, their black coat tails blowing in the wind.

They scanned the streets with grim faces and screamed at anybody and anything that got in the way.

"Just hurry, for the devil in me, hurry!"

The tycoon was spitting fire. "Go and get it sorted. Remember, I always get what I want."

He was cursing and screaming, driven by avarice and greed. The carriage was speeding along, shaking its contents from left to right. That much so in fact, that with every left-hand bend they mastered, the fat tycoon nearly squashed the poor servant who already felt as sick as a pig. He dared not utter a word of conciliation to the madman, who would not stop ranting and raving.

The minute the coach came flying towards the turtle doves, windows slammed shut in the houses of the dreamy suburb. Foam ran from the horses' mouths, their hooves scraping along the cobble stones, ready to break the fence of the green idyll. The two thugs jumped off the seat and hammered against the door, then they quickly turned around and rushed to help their master off the coach.

The sun had already set above the suburban street. It was suppertime and thus, it took a little while for the old weaver woman to answer the door.

"Whoever hammers against my door like this is no here for a polite request," she said, and buried her hand above her hips.

"Correct, you old hag," answered the tycoon instantly thinking that the little house in front of him would be no match for him. But the reaction of the little old lady somewhat indicated that there was more to it, and that he was now going to find out what.

"How dare you."

It was the voice of the teacher.

She had stepped up to stand next to the old weaver woman. Her eyes gleaming with fire, she made it perfectly clear that no one would get past her and take what everybody had worked for.

The tycoon clicked his fingers. But before his thug could step forward, a dozen strapping lads stepped out of the house, followed by a girl and a boy with a flat cap. And to top it all off, there were children hanging out of all the windows and more appearing from the sides of the house and the garden. It did not take long for them to surround the unwanted guests. The thugs took a step back and even the horses stopped foaming, seemingly not interested in breaking the fence anymore.

The tycoon remained calm. He tried to judge the situation. He was looking for a weak point, but no matter how much he searched for it, it was not there. So, he tried another tactic. *Who is the leader of this pack,* he wondered *The old bag? No. The teacher?* Possibly, but she did not seem dominant enough. *The young girl?* There was something about her. She had pushed past the weaver woman and stood right at the front, as if she were spearheading the mob.

The tycoon grunted like a wild boar set to attack and suddenly, he felt not as calm anymore as he had pretended to be, but this had not gone unnoticed.

The boy took his flat cap off and stepped in front of the girl, and said,

"Get lost!" He had said it mockingly, in a manner where pride was stronger than noble reticence and he wished he had not been so abrupt.

The tycoon stopped, digging deep in his memory, searching all corners of his brain for the moment when that phrase had been used. Adults used these sort of phrases often, but not to him since they wouldn't dare. But these words came from a child's mouth and then it dawned on him.

"You," he suddenly said triumphantly. "So, we meet again."

A broad grin appeared on his fat face.

He grinned because he was convinced that he had found the child's weak spot, and then he grimaced into the crowd. Unable to hide his anger, he stepped back into his carriage without further ado and headed back into town just as fast as he had arrived in the suburb.

He left behind him a sense of relief and a few puzzled faces of those who took the whole scenario as nothing more than a contribution to the day's entertainment, livening up its banalities.

"Let's stick together," someone shouted. "One for all

and all for one", and a choir of voices joined in, repeating the motto, tearing some of the folk in suburbia out of their well-earned sleep.

The choir could be heard as far as the crossroads, and the nightwatchman, who was doing his round lighting the street lanterns, shook his head in bewilderment. Dusk had turned to darkness and silence fell over suburbia. Hours later, the nightwatchman finally reached the turning circle and looked back at his work. He admired the row of lanterns glowing in the dark like a row of pearls and took a flask out of his inside pocket, allowing himself a sip. He took another look and another sip, for then only to disappear into a dark, quiet corner. Leaning against the cold stone wall, he wished for the night to change into daylight, for all he really wanted was to go home.

I know what to do, he thought. *I, the oldest night watchman in town.*

He pulled his hat deeper over his face and stood his collar up. He hated being disturbed whilst conducting his work. He took another sip and then, thinking *what the heck,* he emptied the rest of the flask in one go. He sank to the floor, leaning against the wall like a sack of grain that had been deposited there. Not even the stars and the shutters rattling in the wind could disturb his drunken peace.

Thus, he did not notice a shadow sneaking past, avoiding the light and coming to a halt not far from the turtle doves.

Shortly thereafter, if you listened carefully, you could have heard a sigh of relief. And then, watching even more carefully, you would have been able to see the shadow heading straight for the window where the boy had laid his head to rest.

Well, the boy may well have been resting, but asleep he was not. He was mulling over the strange encounter with the tycoon, and it was stopping him from dozing off.

"Boy, are you there?" a frightened, almost terrified voice sounded.

The dark shadow did not want to knock on the glass, but he did notice a little gap and could feel the warm air coming from the room. So, he opened the shutter of the window and peered through the gap.

His whispers flooded through the room, finding an ear. Something nestled, then yawned leisurely, glad that the bad thoughts had suddenly been wiped away. The other children were fast asleep. The boy, however, pushed his duvet aside and looked for his pants. He did not want to hurry even though the whispers urged him to be quick, and when he finally arrived at the window, still half asleep, he could only just stop the shadow leaving.

"Wait," he begged. "Please."

Nothing moved.

Suddenly, a white glove appeared and rested on the windowsill, followed by a barrage of hastily whispered words, tremulous and vulnerable. The boy had to sharpen his senses to understand what the wind was trying to blow away. But then the wind turned leeward, and the boy understood.

"Is this you? The boy with the flat cap?" the shadowed figure asked.

"Yes," answered the boy expectantly.

"The child from the valley, the son of the last fre farmer standing?"

The boy didn't quite understand and pushed hi ear further to the shadow, as far as possible. His stomacl churned. He had this funny feeling that he would soon b part of something big, and his heart started beating loude and louder—and now he clearly understood every wor that came from the shadow's mouth, hearing himself sa that he had understood clearly before he pressed his lip together, clenching all the muscles that would listen t him. And then he heard it loud and clear:

"Listen to what I have to tell you, boy. Liste carefully. Listen as if your life and that of your loved one is on the line." A passing cloud released the moon from th darkness and the boy found himself staring straight int the face of the tycoon's servant. "Listen as if your life i in great danger, and trust me, because it is..." the servan confirmed and sighed heavily.

"It is indeed."

CHAPTER 14

Action

The time to act is now

The servant was searching for the last bit of soul left in him underneath that hard shell that had built up over the years. He had been told to set to work on a series of letters carrying the tycoon's seal. The beautiful round script of the hand that wrote it disguised the seriousness of things to come.

"Up for bludgeon," the headline stated. Two places were to be targeted. One in the valley and one in the suburb. No holding back it stated, not if you want a gold coin for payment.

The servant had folded the letters and sealed them into waterproof envelopes—envelopes just as rough as their recipients.

"Hire the capo and his thugs, and every other thug

you can find between here and the port," the tycoon had thundered. "They better be fast and precise in their work. People need to be taught a lesson. You got that?"

That was an order and not a question, and the servant had immediately sent for the fastest couriers in town, for them to stand by for delivery first thing in the morning. He continued his preparations, looked down at the pile of letters, but all he could think of were those innocent children. He did not know why, but his stomach suddenly churned and he almost fell to the floor. His legs wobbled and then it came to him: *If I let it happen, there will be nowhere for me to hide in this town. No hole to crawl into, not even a little one. Not in this life – and not in the next.*

And so, he fought with his thoughts and contemplated his feelings until his heart brought his head back to reality. In his mind he found himself gazing into the big innocent eyes of the children and then he felt how his soul finally set free the last bit of compassion it had. The very last bit.

I cannot let this happen, he thought and cursed the day he had taken up service with a man who came second to none to the devil. *I simply cannot let this happen!* By then, the clock had already chimed midnight. He ran to the stable and saddled a horse.

Back in the suburb the boy grasped the situation straight away.

"How long have I got?" he asked.

"Half a day. If that," answered the servant.

The boy was chewing his nails in the absence of a pencil, a twig or a straw.

"Wait," he said and disappeared into the dark. The

wind had turned westerly, and the servant looked for his horse. He had tied it up in a dark corner, for it not to be seen. *Hopefully, the stable boy will be asleep and not notice that a horse has gone missing,* he thought. *And the gate, did I close it, or did I leave it open? What if someone raises the alarm and they are sending a search party? What if they issue a bounty for my head? But then again, why would they? I'm nothing to them.*

Aw, well, he thought, *you are bound to have to pay for your sins one day. And if I have to pay, then sooner rather than later.*

Someone pulled at his sleeve. It gave him a fright, and he turned around—it was the boy. He pulled himself together; it was only a boy after all. A boy who should have been shaking, but he wasn't.

The boy was calm and composed and informed the servant about his plans; thus, for that night and the next half of a day, he made the servant one of his helpers.

A silver lining appeared on the horizon and the wind finally turned northerly. They felt it on their backs as they galloped past the turning circle and almost tore the nightwatchman out of his deepest dreams. The boy held onto the servant as best as he could, digging his fingers into the skinny skeleton to stop himself from falling off the horse racing away.

A four-foot fall would most certainly have been the end. They almost flew down the streets, the reins loose, their thighs flat against the flanks of the sweating animal. Their eyes and that of the horse stared straight ahead. As they raced past the houses the fronts of stone and steel melted into a blurred mass. There was no distinction between town, sky and nature, only determination to achieve.

Every thought of failure vanished and with it, any memory of previous pain.

"Ho," the servant sounded, and the horse stopped in its tracks. The servant was exhausted and to be honest so was the horse; its hooves were sore as by now it had lost all its iron horseshoes. It was early morning when they stopped in front of the bank, the ten storey high glass palace in the magnificent avenue.

"Try and delay the couriers as long as you possibly can," requested the boy. "That's all you can do." He slid off the horse without bidding the servant farewell. But he stroked the neck of the brave animal and watched for just a moment as they disappeared down the street. Then he walked straight through the big portal and the booking hall, where a couple of cashiers added up numbers, even though there was nothing to add up. The offices on the first floor were no different. Piles of folders everywhere covered in a thick layer of dust. A graph on the blackboard in the meeting room showed the highest point on the left which then fell to the ground in a zig-zaggy sort of line.

Over in the corner a tipped-over chair, almost as if it had thrown out its occupant to ease the departure. Coin-counting machines stood unused, same as ink well and quills. The boy took it all in, more subconscious than conscious and if a hint of judgement ever arose, it disappeared with the clinking of a cup and a saucer.

I must not lose time, he suddenly thought and took his

cap off, rolling it together whilst he was still running up the stairs. Actually, he was almost jumping the stairs two at a time, his lungs pumping as fast as they could, his pulse stable, his voice waiting to be heard.

The banker heard the noise and set this cup back onto his saucer.

Not another argument, he thought, *not this early in the morning.*

The boy appeared in the door frame and all thoughts vanished into thin air.

The banker was pale, as pale as a sheet. He had lost weight, more weight than a healthy body could stand. But when he set eyes on the boy, he smiled in delight and felt the energy rushing back into his ailing body. He offered him a seat and was quite irritated when the boy refused. But only for a brief moment, for then he understood that his former employee had something on his mind, something that must be rather pressing. He knew this feeling from his younger years. It had made him to what he was now.

"I want to swap. A worthwhile swap," the boy said in a serious voice. "An everlasting swap is what I have to offer."

He clapped his hands and rubbed them together. Not to convince the banker, but to sum up courage. And then he explained the deal as fast as his lips would let him, witnessed by the portrait on the wall, the founder, he who stood above it all and who seemed to give everything around him a lesser meaning. On the frame were gold letters, freshly polished and sealed in wax. They gleamed at the last of the line, so that he would not forget his place in this world.

"Omnia in aeternum," the banker sang. "Everything for eternity." He took his cup and gulped the drink down right to the last drop. The feeling of the warmth of the porcelain took him back to better days. The thought was invigorating, just like the warmth of the sun. The banker had always been passionate about warmth and all life anew and because his heart could not take any more darkness, he finally popped the question. The question signalling the way forward.

"Where to?"

He rang for his butler, who arrived at once, bowed for his master and happily glanced across the room over to the boy.

"To the origin of time," answered the boy, pointing to the empty streets outside. Minutes later, they rushed along the avenue, the carriage taking the bends as if gliding along a steel track.

They arrived at the cuckoo clock about the same time as the couriers were gathering at the tycoon's residence. They were stocky men, with dark weathered faces, their horses chosen for speed. They had even left their carriers at home. Instead, they wore long quivers running across their backs. The horses snorted just as impatiently as the tycoon who was supervising the goings-on.

"Where is he? That useless…" he cried and meant his servant who had run to get the letters but was deliberately buying time. "Go and get him," he screamed at his other staff, who stormed through the corridors looking for the servant who began to realise that his time was up.

That very same moment, the boy knocked on the door of the cuckoo clock.

The clockmaker opened up. He had not changed one bit. The grey hair, the white coat, the little magnifying glasses and the flicker of the obsessed – had he found a way to stop time? The boy did not want to dismiss the thought, but then he heard the *ticking* and the *tocking*, and got straight to the point. The astonished and now also excited clockmaker took the pale guest into the workshop, and the boy shut the door behind them from the outside. If there was a magical spark, then it should not be disturbed by anything in this world. The wait, however, was quite tormenting. It almost tore the boy apart. It played with his nerves until they would stretch no more.

"Next time, I will send the dogs for you," the tycoon raged.

The couriers moved restlessly in their saddles as the servant handed the letters over one by one. The first horse had already gone, galloping at high speed for it had the longest way to go, heading to the valley and back. The next one followed suit, four pubs and some barracks to deliver to. Another was heading for the port and another towards the industrial quarter to find the thugs with the shaven heads.

The only ones now remaining were a grinning tycoon and a bunch of confused aides.

"That's all I could do," the servant mumbled quietly to himself. "That was really all I could do."

The boy could hear the hooves thundering through the streets. *Maybe I am just imagining it,* he thought just as he caught glimpse of a black rider galloping past the cuckoo clock. His heart missed a beat.

It is too late, he thought. Far too late. He looked at the collection of timepieces that kept on running without him being able to do anything about it. Another rider flew past, and the boy sensed the danger. It almost felt as if it was the end.

I am losing it, he thought. *Everything around me will be lost. The girl, the weaver woman, the teacher, mother and father, my siblings and my friends—I'll not be able to protect them from what I've conjured. I hate the tycoon; I hate the town.*

"Do not bear a grudge, child," I said. "Think about the swap, only the swap and nothing else."

He thought about the swap but was not able to hear what was said in the workshop. The spoken word was unable to penetrate through the thick oak door. And what little he believed to have understood was drowned out by the *ticking* and *tocking* of the clocks all around him.

The boy pressed his ear against the door.

Not a chance. Not on your nelly. He did not see the thugs with their baseball bats in their hands as they walked through the alley. But the butler did, and he reminded everyone that it was time.

"They are not here for us," the boy shouted, and wished that it were the case. "They are here for them."

A head full of ginger hair poked through the door. When it set eyes on the boy, it lifted the bat. A fist struck hard from behind, straight between the shoulder blades and caused the head to stumble off.

"Come on," barked a voice from afar. "You can play in the suburb."

At the same time, a heartfelt *No* sounded from the workshop. It had penetrated the thick oak door and the boy had turned around, full of disappointment, and he could envisage himself sitting by the oak tree, all alone, knocking at doors that remained closed. He envisaged himself walking once again endlessly through wetness and cold, with bleeding feet, running from something that haunted him.

He could see himself flat out in the water, drifting down the river, below the surface, his open eyes screaming for his mother who would not answer. Hiding until it was dark because the whole world had turned against him. And he could hear the whispers, imagined the pointing fingers, the hate and the shame, so bad and so painful that everything had turned to stone. But because he had already experienced some of life's hardships, it had given him strength.

So he shrugged his bad thoughts off the way he had always done, because deep inside, he had already grown into a young man. And he opened the door just as the deal was done.

"On the highest tower in town?" the banker asked. He was holding the right hand of the clockmaker. The left hand was lying on the man's shoulder.

Eternity was up for grabs and he had no intention of letting it pass.

"The cathedral, of course," answered the clockmaker. "High up. That is what she was designed for."

He had built her for that and only that. He knew i
and so did the banker now.

"I will pay you what you are due," the banker said
"what you deserve for your work of excellence and for you
pride."

The clockmaker took off his glasses and leaned
against his workbench. He looked satisfied and happy. Thi
was the beginning of a special time, a golden period so to
speak, and he knew that his life's work had been fulfilled
and he would not have to touch another clock again unti
the day he died.

Dark figures kept stumbling past the windows, a
first just a few but then more and more. Droves of them
in small groups and large crowds. The boy held his breath
He wanted to barge into the conversation but decided to
bide his time.

The banker looked at him and took a deep breath.

"Now let us talk about your share," he said to the boy
"The warehouse, the mill, the silos and the carts shall al
belong to the farmers of the valleys, just as discussed. I an
happy for them to take them over."

And as he spoke, he drew a cross on his chest usin;
his finger, a sign to seal the deal.

Then he continued:

"And the debt registers belonging to the tycoon?
will throw those out."

The tower clock and all other clocks chimed fo
midday almost as if they were ringing in the finale.

The eternal one hissed.

"Actually, they will be flying into the gutter righ

away as a sign of his ruin for now and evermore. I can get over the loss and I am happy to fund it, because this swap makes it worth my while."

The boy danced in delight.

He almost touched the ceiling doing a jump for joy. And when his feet hit the ground, he turned and stormed out into the street, shouting, "The tycoon is bankrupt. The tycoon is bankrupt. Listen up and tell everyone."

Not a soul stirred with the information, apart from the butler who suddenly understood.

"The tycoon is bankrupt," they both shouted in unison until the windows and the doors opened and people began to congregate on the streets.

They started to whisper, intrigued about the news that had just come to light. Then one of them laughed, a big belly laugh.

"The tycoon? Bankrupt? That means he hasn't got a pot to pee in. Just like me."

He slapped his thighs, roaring with laughter. The laughter caught on and broke through the town, it roared through the streets, the lanes and the alleys. It sounded through all the windows and doors and finally even caught up with the thugs, the shaven heads, the couriers in town, suburb and valley.

The thug with the ginger hair turned a corner. He threw his bat away and flared his nostrils. The other thugs followed suit. They found themselves approached by a rider dressed all in black. No one rushed or bullied anymore, but the look on their faces indicated that they wanted their dues. They headed straight for the tycoon's villa.

Arriving at the villa, everyone was in uproar, with the first bailiffs already demanding access. But to no avail. There was anger brewing outside the door. The cooks, maids and stable boys sensed this and grabbed what they could and disappeared by the back door before it was too late. Only the manservant decided to stay.

He wanted to see his master fall, even if it would mean his own downfall. But this feeling quickly disappeared when his master made an entrance on the spiral staircase. As he towered above the head of his servant, his height and weight still signalling a brutal appearance, the servant froze.

He was embarrassed by his own cowardice, even though he should not have been, just like a hunter feels regret looking at his freshly shot deer. He pulled himself together and took a brave step towards the door, opening the first bolt.

"Don't," stuttered the tycoon, "Please don't," and he tumbled down the stairs with a facial expression that begged for salvation. The servant saw himself affirmed in his actions and opened the second bolt, pushing it noisily into place.

The tycoon dropped to his knees, begging for mercy. He pulled out the golden case and placed it at the bottom of the servant's feet, adding a ring, his pocket watch and anything else he could find in his pockets that was of value.

But the servant ignored the gesture.

The third bolt was pushed back with a loud click and the door finally opened. Anger permeated into the house and the hall. The servant fell to the floor, trampled down by the angry masses. The tycoon rolled sideways and hid behind a curtain. He did not see how the angry mob trashed his formidable mansion, nor did he care. He crawled on all fours towards the hidden servant's entrance, followed the passage towards the kitchen and finally pushed himself through the half-open French doors. He got out by the skin of his teeth. He stumbled towards the stable, losing a shoe in the process and minutes later, if one watched closely, one would have noticed a rider galloping off the premises. The tycoon had disappeared in a cloud of dust, far into the horizon, never to be seen again.

CHAPTER 15

Departure

Depart with determination, arrive with a smile

I last saw the boy, as he was standing under the old oak tree again. This time clothed in a suit of the finest cloth, his boots shining brightly in the autumn light. A silk scarf held off the first autumn chill with the flat cap sitting proudly on his head.

He knew that this last part of the journey would be the easiest. He walked over to the carriage and tightened the load. He had brought with him the harvest of the summer just gone, barrels, crates, and sacks full of goodies. And with him, the girl, smiling broadly with her brother by her side.

She smiled at him through loving eyes and the boy felt butterflies in his stomach every time he looked at her. *Amazing what we have been through,* he thought. Then hi thoughts turned to home and he tried to guess how far they still had to go.

I will get there by evening, he said to himself. *Definitely. And we will be pleased to see each other. It's been a long time.*

I must not show despair when I set eyes on them. They have been through a lot, just like all the others in the valley. Their hollow cheeks and deep wrinkles will tell the tale. I must not show any grief; instead, I will smile, the best and most honest smile there is. Then they will understand that those bad times are finally behind them, and with it the pain they have had to endure.

He could hear a happy whistle coming down the country lane. The strapping lads had finally caught up. Soon, the trek of home comers would be complete.

The boy used the time to walk over to the oak once more. He needed a moment by himself. He could see the town on the horizon, high up in the north. Some of the furnaces had fired up again, just a couple for now, but they signalled the end of the storm. *Another year and everything will be forgotten,* thought the boy. *The town will be grinding and groaning and sweating again, just like it did on the day of my arrival. But all will be well,* he thought.

The weaver woman and the teacher will see to that and they will continue to look after the orphans and strays and all those that need care and protection. That is what the little paradise is for and they will take good care of it.

It will always be my home from home, especially if we need to return to the town. Until then, there will be plenty of hard work to get on with in the valley. But with what we know and what we have and what the banker has granted us to make a start, we will see the day when the valleys will rise again.

"And that will be soon. Very soon," said the boy, and looked over to his friends.

"Let's go," the girl called over to him and held out her hand.

"Come on, little scruff bag."

The boy smiled. He took his hand and for a brief moment, pressed it against the rough, but soft bark of this magnificent tree, just to remind himself that all of this wasn't a dream. I knew that my presence was no longer needed. I had become a part of it all.

Part of all the children who travelled towards the valleys on this glorious autumn day. There was still a lot of sorrow that had to be addressed in all the corners of our beautiful, but sometimes mean and difficult world. Before I parted company with him, I asked him,

"What will you do… what will you do if someone comes and ruins everything you hold dear?"

The boy turned round and looked at the girl.

"What will you do if someone pulls the floor away from beneath your feet whilst you are up and running achieving and swapping, and when time runs away almost as if the hourglass has broken?"

A breeze blew through the crown of the magnificent old oak tree, and a red and golden leaf floated gently from the tree onto the boy's shoulder. He took his flat cap off and ran his fingers through his hair.

"And if your world caves in," I said, "what will you do then?"

The boy looked up, full of determination. He put the

cap back on his head and jumped onto the seat of the cart.

He took the reins and said with a very loud voice,

"If that happens, Courage my dear friend, if that ever happens, then I will just create a new one."

CHAPTER 16

Homecoming

The most beautiful day

The people in the valley did not anticipate what this day would bring. They were busy preparing for the winter. The staff at the trading post had disappeared from one day to the next, without forewarning, leaving a vast chaos behind them.

But no one cared. Everybody was just relieved that they had won back their independence. They returned to the fields and tried to harvest what had been left behind. Some of the fields lay fallow, for the overseer had stopped planting seeds months ago when the town had been adversely affected by the economic crisis. The produce coming from the valley was simply too expensive and it was a struggle to sell. At that point the tycoon had instructed the overseer to turn every penny around twice, and this he had done. He had reduced production, much to the detriment of the residents of the valley, who once again had to worry about how they would survive the winter.

There was great worry in the minds of the people, but as long as the autumn climate remained mild, they knew that they had a good chance. However, if the frost returned as it had in the past, life would be hard. Very hard indeed.

No one even noticed the faint rumble coming from the south. The sun had started setting on the horizon, throwing long shadows towards the mountains. The rumble grew louder and louder, accompanied by the neighing of horses to the rhythm of a group of children singing a joyful song. The convoy had reached the cross roads. It was time to say farewell, even if it wasn't forever. The strapping lads and two of the wagons would carry on into one of the side valleys.

The girl and her little brother moved to another wagon which would take them further east towards a little lake where a row of houses lined a small creek. Another group was heading for the forest at the edge of the mountains. They still had quite a way to go and thus started pressuring the others for a quick departure.

The children all bid farewell, hugging one another and wishing each other well. They vowed to get together as soon as time would allow, for they had become good friends throughout their journey.

As far as the boy and the girl were concerned, theirs was more than a friendship. They both felt it deep in their hearts as they looked into each other's eyes. They'd already started counting down the time until they were due to meet again.

With a sudden "hooray," the convoy departed. Th
boy, now all by himself, watched his horses as they trotte
along. They had once stood in the barn of the tycoon, an
upon their master's bankruptcy had fallen into the hand
of the banker, who in turn had given them, together witl
many other things, to the children.

The boy decided that he would give one of thes
horses to his father's neighbour. He was certain it woul
be much needed for working the fields in summer an
fetching firewood from the forest in winter.

Having finished his thought, the boy looked aroun
and checked his load. There were large sacks of semolina
millet, oats, peas, and rusks. The smaller sacks containe
sugar, salt, and dried fruit. Also on board were severa
boxes of onions, carrots, apples, and pears. And right a
the back, hidden under a few layers of cloth and woo
little oak casks could be found, containing butter, lard
and cheese. Air dried sausages and bacon, as well as spice
from countries far afield, had not been forgotten. A littl
bit of everything, but plenty to go round and share witl
the neighbours.

And of course, the boy had brought presents for thos
he held dear. He wanted to bring personal joy to each an
every one of them. He reached under his seat and pulle
out a large jute bag. I set off with one of these, only mucl
smaller, he thought. Filled with just a few apples and nothin;
else. Not even enough for a couple of days. And now I an
returning with a cuddly donkey for my little brother. H
couldn't help but grin; just the thought of his little brother'

eyes made him smile already. And of course, he wouldn't be so little any more. He thought of the three silk scarfs he had chosen for his mother and his two sisters, neatly folded and stashed away in the jute bundle. He could already see them twirling with joy in front of his eyes, his father clapping his hands in delight. "Oh father," he whispered. "Of course, I have thought of you too. I have brought you a pair of winter boots unlike any you have ever owned before. These are hob nailed and lined with sheepskin. You will be able to climb up the highest mountains without slipping and they will keep your feet dry and warm, even in the deepest snow or the heaviest sleet."

The boy had many more thoughts and continued smiling as he drove along. He did not look left nor right and almost did not notice that he had already turned the last corner. His father's house was standing right in front of him.

His father had just stepped outside the barn on his way to fetch hay for the very few animals they still had left. He looked at the wagon and into the young man's face and sank to the ground. His mother, who had witnessed his arrival from the kitchen window where she sat catching the last rays of daylight mending some clothes, instantly dropped her needlework and ran to the door in disbelief. She cried for joy, which in turn alarmed his two sisters who appeared from the sitting room and ran towards their brother, happy that their luck was back.

The boy jumped off the wagon. He didn't even feel his feet touching the ground. All he saw was the happily glowing faces of his parents and his siblings and wide-open arms. Moments later he felt kisses on his face and tears. Tears of joy. He felt the gentle hands of his mother embracing him and his father patting him on the back at the same time.

Suddenly the welcome was interrupted by a loud squeak. The boy looked up to see his second eldest sister returning with his little brother. Only he was not quite so little any more. He was walking now, even running, albeit not as fast as one would have expected on this occasion. Instead, he squeaked as loud as he could and made himself known within the safety of his sister's arms. The family was complete.

Time almost stood still that evening, just as the clockmaker had once foretold. It was one of those unforgettable moments that happens when good things come together, a moment that will stick forever in your mind. It let the sadness of the past years fade and proved the clockmaker right again. "Time will heal all wounds, my dear boy," said the mother as she stroked his hair.

They stood close together until the horses became restless and fretted to be freed from their bridle gear. They put the horses into the barn and began unloading the wagon. It was difficult to stash all the treasures away in the little house. "We need more space and a stable," the father said, deep in thought. The boy nodded. He looked at his father and noticed that his face did not seem as gaunt anymore. The deep wrinkles on his mother's forehead had also smoothed out. It seemed that the time of hardship and worry had finally come to an end.

It wasn't until the sun had set behind the mountain

that they finally finished their work. As they gathered around the big family table, the boy lit the old ornate oil lamp and, much to everyone's delight, he started handing out the presents he had selected with much care. No one thought about going to bed that night. Even the little brother would not tire. He was far too busy playing with his little toy donkey. He showed him the whole house. The sisters wore their new silk scarves, feeling like princesses. "They fit perfectly," shouted the father as he took the first steps in his new boots. As the mother admired the pretty pattern on her silk scarf, a thought crossed her mind of how lucky they were to have such a fine son and brother. How lucky that he had found his way home and we are all back together again. It seemed that all the kisses she blew to the moon had not been in vain. But how did he do it?

"How did you do it, boy?" the father asked as if he had read the mother's mind. The room went quiet and everyone looked at the boy, awaiting his answer.

"How did I do it?" the boy repeated. He knew that short question would take a long time to answer. He took a pencil from his pocket and stuck it between his lips. He leaned his head back and pushed the pencil from side to side. A picture began to take shape in his head, a bit blurry at first, but then it grew sharper and sharper. A picture of the people he had encountered on his journey. The weaver woman and the clockmaker and many other faces he had learned to appreciate over time.

The pencil in his mouth started picking up speed. It only stopped once for a brief moment and then it continued again. His family, eagerly awaiting his answer, remained silent. The boy shut his eyes and the penci stopped. He could see it clearly now. The picture of hi journey, his luck. He opened his eyes, removed the penci from his lips, and said with a big smile:

"We have all been given five treasures in life that w need to hold dear. Treasures that tell us, through the lacl of them or through abundance, how easy our journey i going to be."

He held out his hand and counted on his fingers: "Th first is health, the second is time, the third is knowledge the fourth is family and friends, and the fifth is wealth."

"Some of these treasures are more important thar others," he said. "Some of them are finite; others wil accumulate," he continued. "Some will quickly disappea if you don't look after them. The secret is to get the balanc right and shift between them as the journey through lif requires. One must use one's wisdom."

"Shift?" he heard one of his sisters say.

"Yes," answered the boy. "Every human longs fo something and every human also has something to give All you need to do is find out what you want, and you mus be prepared to give for it. The weaver woman, for instance did not want to be alone. So we kept her company, anc she gave us her paradise. The young miss always wanted tc be a teacher, not a librarian; she taught us all to read anc write. The clockmaker wished for a fitting place to han; his masterpiece and remuneration to see him through hi retirement. The banker wanted to be remembered, so brought them both together and, in the end, everyone wa able to fulfill their dreams. Even us children."

"And the tycoon?" asked the mother with slight concern.

"He also got what he was due," answered the boy. "He had taken from everyone, and all he had to give was fear, sorrow and misery. Those who are driven by greed will, sooner or later, all encounter the same fate. They bring it upon themselves."

The boy would have been able to explain a lot more of what makes the difference between happiness and misery. Bravery to start with, and sticking together, no matter how bad things are. He did however mention the storm, how a bad situation opened a new opportunity and how important it is to have friends who think and feel the same.

He had a lot more to say, but there was plenty of time. Right now, he just wanted to enjoy the moment. He wanted to absorb the happiness and lock it deep into his heart, for these valuable memories would shine forever more. He did not want to look back to the dark times but look forward to the bright shining light. He felt another kiss on his forehead, and how the hand of his mother squeezed his own.

He suddenly had a beautiful thought, but he kept it to himself.

He had found another treasure and most probably the biggest secret of all on the journey through life.

To know why you are doing it …

Thank you

...for reading THE BRAVE CHILD: A tale about the treasures in life. If you enjoyed this book, please leave a brief review on Amazon.

Finally, I want to wish you all the best on your journey. May you find the treasures that you long for, just as the nameless boy did and may Courage be your companion, wherever you go...

Sincerely,

Andreas

Printed in Great Britain
by Amazon

13374372R00121